Learn what it really means to serve Christ.

Colleen Townsend Evans began her study of The Beatitudes because of a need in her own life. *"I longed to be more deeply Christian where it counted, but I needed help."* She found that help in Jesus' gospel of love — The Beatitudes. In *A New Joy,* which sold 225,000 copies, she shared her life-changing discoveries and inspired women throughout the world.

Life in the 1980s presents its own unique challenges to Christian women, who still need to experience the relevance of The Beatitudes in their everyday lives. In *A Deeper Joy,* Colleen Townsend Evans returns to The Beatitudes and extensively updates her original text. Her understanding will provide you with new insights on the true meaning of life, love, sex, and commitment. Her workable, practical suggestions and deeply personal anecdotes bring help to all women seeking an effective, fulfilling ministry to their families and their world.

"I chose them [The Beatitudes] because in these words Jesus was speaking to believers like me—they weren't very pious, and they were far from perfect, but they had decided for Jesus. Now they needed His help in trying to live the life to which He had called them."

(continued on back flap)

A Deeper Joy

A Deeper Joy

Colleen Townsend Evans

A REVELL/MERIT PUBLICATION

FLEMING H. REVELL COMPANY

Old Tappan, New Jersey
Publisher

MERIT BOOKS, INC.

Flourtown, Pennsylvania
Producer

Material in this volume previously appeared under the title *A New Joy*. Unless otherwise identified, Scripture quotations are from THE NEW TESTAMENT IN MODERN ENGLISH (Revised Edition), translated by J. B. Phillips. © J. B. Phillips 1958, 1960, 1972. Used by permission of Macmillan Publishing Co., Inc.

Scripture quotations identified KJV are from the King James Version of the Bible.

Scripture quotations marked TLB are taken from *The Living Bible*, copyright © 1971 by Tyndale House Publishers, Wheaton, IL. Used by permission.

Scripture quotations identified RSV are from the Revised Standard Version of the Bible, copyrighted 1946, 1952, © 1972 and 1973.

Excerpts from THE VELVETEEN RABBIT by Margery Williams. Reprinted by permission of Doubleday & Company, Inc.

Library of Congress Cataloging in Publication Data

Evans, Colleen Townsend.
   A deeper joy.

   Encl. and updated ed. of: A new joy. [1973]
   1. Title.
BT382.E55   1982   248.8'43   82–3732
ISBN 0–8007–1306–0   AACR2

Contents

6

Preface

For me, a book that has been personally therapeutic is like someone who has played a significant role for good in my life. From time to time I need to return and get in touch with that person—I suppose, to see if the old power is still there.

A New Joy—the writing of it—was that kind of book for me; so I have returned, this time to read, to update here and there, and once again to let the teaching from the Beatitudes speak to my everyday life.

So I am going to begin at the very beginning:

I have just come in from a walk along the beach. It was cold today, so my nose is red, and my body tingles. What a wonderful, beautiful feeling!

Walking the beach is something I love, but that isn't all. I need it. It isn't something I do every day for exercise. No, I save the beach for days when I need the sea's ministry. For there are times when I need the wind—like the wind of the Spirit—to blow the cobwebs from my mind and let me think more clearly. And there are times when the vastness of the sea reminds me of the vastness of God's love, and the tide's ebb and flow of His dependability.

One night I walked the beach until dawn, seeking the strength I needed to face surgery—for some reason a thing I found particularly difficult at that time. *Why?* I asked myself. Then the words of my doctor-friend came to my mind, giving me a clue: "I think we'll find everything in good order, Coke, but we can't be sure."

It was fear, not of surgery but of the unknown, that tormented me. Over and over I told myself it was a common enough fear, but it numbed me. Release came only when I allowed myself to remember that God can even be—can *especially* be—trusted with the unknowns of our lives.

How many times my husband, Lou, and I have been drawn to the sea when we needed guidance on specific issues in our church or in our own lives. We realize that God is everywhere and always within our reach, so that we don't have to go to a particular place to talk to Him. It's just that we can get away from life's distractions when we walk the quiet beach where nothing interrupts our conversation. It isn't God who needs the silence—*we* do.

So it has gone—walks, too many to count, during these past several years when we have had the privilege of living alongside the sea. And so it was today. I needed to think, to sort things out in my mind, for I had been asked a question I didn't know how to answer.

When a person writes a book, he usually includes a preface explaining the purpose of the book. Well, I had written a book, and now Fleming H. Revell Company, my publishers, asked me for a preface. In other words, my readers would be asking me, "Why did you write this book?" The question was simple enough. Not so the answer.

I suppose I could say I wrote the book because I was asked to. A few years ago I wrote an article for *Guideposts* entitled "Express Your True Feelings." It was based on the Beatitude "Happy are the utterly sincere, for they will see God!" (Matthew 5:8). Revell suggested that I write a book about all the Beatitudes, and I liked the idea. But that isn't the whole story, and the book didn't really begin there.

It began many years ago and certainly not as a book. It was a study, a simple, feeling-level study, that grew out of my own life. In those days I was a young wife and the mother of four little children. Although I had been a Christian only a few years, my life had been very glowing and exciting—up to that time. But with the responsibilities and work of a family comes fatigue, and one morning I woke up wondering where the glow had gone.

I began to think back a few years, searching for an answer. Yes, it was there all right; at first I could see it dimly, but gradually the visibility improved.

For several years before I married Louie I had worked in the motion-picture industry. I thoroughly enjoyed my career, especially the people with whom I worked. During those years I also became a very enthusiastic believer in Jesus Christ. To me it didn't seem unusual that a spiritual rebirth should happen to someone in my profession: I have known, and still know, many dedicated Christians in the motion-picture industry. But to many people the combination of my belief and my profession had a special attraction. Because of that I was often asked to speak to various groups, telling them how Christ came into my life. Even after I left my motion-picture work for my "other career," the one I wanted more, the speaking invitations continued.

Because I have always been eager to share my faith, I said yes to as many requests as I could, although speaking was not then (and is not now) a thing I leap toward with joy. Eventually the pressure became uncomfortable because I allowed myself to be influenced by a few people who felt that it was not only my opportunity but my duty to speak about Jesus publicly.

Yes, I could see where the glow had gone. It had retreated deep inside me. I was beginning to feel like an "up front" Christian, and obviously I was resisting the celebrity bit. It is one thing to talk about being a Christian in front of groups, but quite another to be a Christian in your home and in your community. I longed to be more deeply Christian where it really counted, but I needed help.

God has a marvelous sense of timing. At the very moment when I really needed it, I decided to join a women's Bible-study group in the new church we were starting in Bel Air, California. I did it simply to learn more about the Bible, never expecting that it would offer me anything more.

Our group met once a week, exploring several different methods of studying the Bible. Then, after dealing with the historical and theological background of a passage, we were asked to rewrite it in our own words, forgetting everything but what the passage meant to each of us, personally. As I did that, the Scriptures suddenly became very real. I'll never forget the excitement I felt when I began to see that the Bible could be applied to life today—and especially to *my* life.

But why a book about the Beatitudes? I chose them because in these words Jesus was speaking to believers like me: They weren't very pious, and they were far from perfect, but they had decided *for* Jesus. Now they needed His help in trying to live the life to which He had called them.

Help is exactly what you will find in the Beatitudes, for here is where Jesus spells out His gospel of love. He tells us what love is, how it feels, and what it does. Instead of listing laws and commandments, He explains how our inner motivations and heart responses can either help us express love or get in its way. Specifically, practically, and in such a down-to-earth manner, Jesus gets to the core of the Christian life.

That was what I needed several years ago, and so my study of the Beatitudes began. I wanted to find out what these beautiful words meant when Jesus spoke them almost two thousand years ago—and what they might mean to me, a woman living in our complicated modern world.

I immersed myself in Matthew 5, eventually becoming familiar with the Sermon on the Mount in every translation I could find. Gradually I could feel what it must have been like to be in that crowd of believers at Jesus' feet. I could see myself among them as I wrote a paraphrase of what I thought Jesus might have said to me had I been alone with Him. Finally, and perhaps more important than anything else, I prayed that the *attitudes* Jesus described might become a part of me, from the inside out.

Because it helps me to write down my thoughts and feelings, I began to record the practical applications of the Beatitudes as they came to me. Sometimes they would come during moments of meditation and prayer, but more often they came unexpectedly as I was rushing from place to place doing my thing for the day. So this book has been written on scraps of paper as I waited for the car pool to take my children to school or as I took my turn as driver and waited outside the school, on the program for a play, or on the back of a church bulletin when I was struck with an idea in church. (Forgive me, Louie!) My children are now teenagers, and therefore the jottings shared here cover the musings and feelings of years.

But—back to the question I considered as I walked the beach this morning. Why did I write this book at all? By now you know, just as I do. I wrote it out of my own need. I wrote it because I have found the Bible—and here, specifically, the Beatitudes—to be real and vital to me, a woman living today. I am sharing in this way because during the past few years I have learned that sharing our needs, our struggles, our joys, our affirmations, our love—in short, sharing ourselves—can be one of life's richest experiences. So I am receiving perhaps more than my share.

If, through this book, I can help one woman discover that Jesus Christ is real and that His Word is something she can use in her everyday life, I shall be forever grateful.

These pages are not about talking the talk, but

about walking the walk. And now I'll shake the sand from my shoes and get on with it.

It has been almost ten years since I crossed the last *t* on that preface and, with a prayer in my heart, sent it on to Revell. I find it hard to believe: almost a decade. And in those years, much about my life has changed.

For one thing, the children you will read about in this book have grown up, and in their leave-taking, I have learned a valuable lesson about family life: "Letting go" does not diminish love. It enables a growing love to be.

Then, as my husband and I have grown older, we have also grown closer. While we are more distinct as individuals, we are nearer in spirit. As Louie has become more the person God created him to be—as opposed to the person people (including me) wanted, or needed, him to be—I have felt freer to become myself. I am strongly linked, by choice, to my husband, yet separate from him: two, yet one. The years have been a rich journey, leaving us certain that God's relationships are meant to operate according to the law of "increasing return."

No decade can pass without owning its share of pain, and this one has been no exception. I remember writing the chapter on mourning in the original version of this book and wondering how I, who had lost neither mother nor father, could write with credibility about the reality of God's comfort as we mourn the loss of those near to us. So I wrote from what I had seen in the lives of friends and from my faith in what God said He would be to us at such times.

Now I know from experience that what I wrote then—in faith—was true.

Even the setting of our lives has changed. We no longer live in California, by the sea. Louie now serves the National Presbyterian Church, and we live, by choice, in the inner city of Washington, D.C. I still need those walks for my soul, but I have exchanged the white sands of La Jolla for the gray concrete sidewalks of the nation's capital.

Yes, the years have brought change, both within and without. Yet, at the deepest level, so much is still the same. For instance, I am still convinced—as I was when I wrote this book—that *attitude* is at the very core of our Christian life. Our actions spring from our attitudes. Indeed, so powerful are our attitudes, that should they be in conflict with our outward and verbal expressions, they will speak so loudly that people will not be able to hear what we say.

But where best to learn about this hidden power in our lives? A friend of mine has said: "The Beatitudes of Jesus teach us about the 'attitudes that ought to be.' " This surely has been true for me. There is no Scripture passage I go to more often for help in seeking the right attitudes—whatever the situation—than the Sermon on the Mount. And I find myself returning to them more often.

I believe the eighties hold new challenges for everyone, particularly for Christian women. I believe there are potential ministries ahead that will absolutely astound us; and I, for one, am praying these new arenas of service for women will count for Christ. More than anything, I want to be faithful to God in this decade of opportunity. I want to be the woman God means for me to be. I want to bless my family, to befriend especially the poor and powerless in my community, but also those who are burdened with power. I want to serve as Jesus served, with no thought for personal return. But this means all my motivations must originate with—and be kept (right) by—God. It means I must get back to basics—to attitudes—to where it all begins. It means a fresh immersion in the teachings of Jesus as He gave them that day on the mountain.

I must become newly and radically aware of what it is to be:

> poor in spirit—bankrupt without Christ
> meek—gentle, yet strong and full of power
> pure in heart—transparent, a passer-on of light, in
>   my relationships
> merciful—able to give myself lavishly, without ever
>   losing myself to anyone but God
> authentic in mourning—able to accept God's grace
>   and healing for the promised losses and suffering
>   of life and through it all to be the "salty,"
>   "light-filled" woman God intends me to be.

It's all there for me—and for every woman—in the Beatitudes. Just a few simple verses of teaching tucked away in Matthew 5, but they hold the power to change our lives utterly.

This time, as we begin, there is no sand to brush from my feet, just a little inner-city dust and grime. But never mind, I'm excited and eager to be on our way. . . .

A Deeper Joy

1

> ...You must change your hearts and minds—for the kingdom of Heaven has arrived.
>
> Matthew 4:17
>
> ...turn to God, for the Kingdom of heaven is near.
>
> Matthew 4:17 TLB

On Being a Beatitude

The Sermon on the Mount is considered by many to be the greatest ethical teaching ever recorded. In fact, so high are its precepts that some people have deified the Sermon itself—and forgotten the One who preached it. I'm sure you as well as I have heard the remark, "It doesn't matter what you believe about Jesus, as long as you live according to the Sermon on the Mount."

But before we even attempt to understand the teaching, it is absolutely necessary to realize that the Sermon must *never* be separated from Jesus. They belong together. In

19

fact, I believe it is impossible to understand—and *live*—these precepts without having a relationship with Christ. It would be naive and unfair to ask you to try. Apart from Jesus, His sermon is an impossible idealism—a lofty, but very frustrating, ethic.

If, however, you have chosen to be Christ's disciple and walk with Him, then studying and committing yourself to the personal and social power of the Sermon can revolutionize your life. When it comes to faith, the Sermon on the Mount (and for me, specifically, the Beatitudes) is where the rubber hits the road.

To me, the Beatitudes are especially meaningful because they deal with our attitudes, and I have long felt that attitudes are at the center of our lives. They influence everything we do.

Consider family life. It is not where or how a family lives that makes a difference. It is the attitude within—and emanating from—that family that counts. Nothing nourishes a child more than warm, healthy, loving attitudes. To be desired and affirmed as a person is as important to his or her mental and emotional health as food is to physical well-being.

When I was very small, my mother and father were divorced. My mother found it necessary to go to work immediately; and until something could be worked out for my supervision, I was left in the care of my elderly grandfather during the day. He was a good man—a splendid old gentleman—and I felt not only loved by him; I felt cherished. But soon, out of concern for his age—and my "proper care"—I was taken every day to stay with a family across town, where I would get "proper care"; hot regular meals, family atmosphere, and so on. It seemed the right thing to do, and yet in a matter of weeks it was evident something was very wrong. Words told me these good people had taken me in out of the "kindness of their hearts," but what I felt from the family was that they really didn't like doing it very much. The *attitude* I sensed from them was one of duty. I was a burden, not a joy. I became sickly and every evening waited with my face pressed against the window, watching for the first glimpse of my mother coming down the street to take me home. What I really wanted was for mother and me to move back with my grandfather, where he could watch me while mother worked and where we could take care of each other. The "hot meals and proper supervision for a little girl" meant nothing compared to having a grandfather who sat on the front porch, laughing as I did cartwheels and somersaults on his front lawn—whose blue eyes filled with tears as I sang his favorite songs—and who communicated with a telling look or gentle touch that we were pals.

Eventually we did move back with granddad, and I still remember the way his voice choked with tears when we asked him if he wanted us to come home. He didn't speak, but his brimming eyes gave us our answer.

I was from a broken home; we were poor; and yet in many ways I had an enriched childhood: a committed mother who really cared and a grandfather who told me without a word that I brought him joy. Attitude made the difference. I'll always be grateful I was not denied the warmth and affirmation I received, in exchange for three hot meals, hair always brushed, and socks that matched. I was blessed.

It's true: Attitude affects life on every level. Every periodical I read lately seems to have something to say about the importance of the effect of our attitude on our daily life and health. In *Anatomy of an Illness,* Norman Cousins tells what healing power laughter and joy brought to his life. His heartwarming story made the words of Proverbs—"A merry heart does good like a medicine"—ring in my soul for days. Nor is his experience an isolated case. The clinical evidence that positive attitudes of faith, hope, gratitude, generosity, laughter can make us well is growing every day. We humans are more spiritual than physical, it seems, and our bodies are barometers of our inner selves. Mental-health statistics tell us that 90 percent of our ailments have a spiritual-emotional-attitude basis.

In his book *Human Options* Norman Cousins seems to support that claim:

> Nothing is more wondrous about the fifteen billion neurons in the human brain than their ability to convert thoughts, hopes, ideas, and attitudes into chemical substances. Everything begins, therefore, with belief. What we believe is the most powerful option of all.

Later in the same book, the author adds:

> It makes no sense to believe that only the negative emotions have an effect on the body's chemistry. Every emotion, negative or positive, makes its registrations on the body's systems.

Speaking directly to this matter of our body's systems in *There's a Lot More to Health Than Not Being Sick,* Bruce Larson

refers to the new, and still very costly, miracle drug inter-
feron—a possible cure for all kinds of diseases from the
common cold to cancer. It seems the body has the capacity
for manufacturing this drug, but not enough or at the
needed time. Bruce writes:

> Right now the experts are looking for less costly
> ways to produce synthetic interferon. I wish them
> success, but I would rather see us working toward
> increasing the release of our natural interferon
> through the practice of positive attitudes, spiritual
> values, or disciplines of the mind.

When I was on my way from Washington to California
recently, I was glancing through the airline magazine, and
there it was again, in an article on aging: *"The single most
important* factor in staying alive and alert is to stay plugged
in to society—maintaining mental involvement and a *positive attitude."* And from another study: "Energy level is
more a matter of attitude than age."

The evidence is staggering: In terms of mental and physical health, attitude makes the difference. This doesn't mean
we ignore the physical, but that we accept the influence of
our attitudes on our health.

It may seem that by emphasizing the influence of our
attitudes, we are neglecting the importance of our actions.
Not so. I truly believe that our attitudes confirm or negate
our good works; they shout at people before our words can
be heard or our deeds seen. Attitudes are like shadows;
they accompany us wherever we go. We cannot hide them.

In Gabriel Marcel's play *A Man of God* Edmee is a guilt-
ridden wife ruled by her unhealthy attitudes. Another char-

acter in the play describes her this way: "Edmee is so aus-
tere, so wrapped up in her duties . . . so absorbed in good
work . . . it gives me the impression of a sleep-walker. I
sometimes feel Edmee is going through life half conscious."

Edmee created a mood that spoke louder than her actions. We all do. We create a mood when we enter a room;
when we sit next to someone at church, on a bus; or even
as we catch someone's eye as we pass by.

The mood we create is the spirit that comes from within,
and spirit and attitude are as closely related as two sides of
a coin. Attitude therefore becomes crucial to the disciple,
and the attitude is the focal point of the Beatitudes.

Perhaps this is why I feel it is important not only to study
the Beatitudes, but to immerse our lives in them, to feed
on them daily.

In the beginning of the Sermon on the Mount, Jesus
speaks about our actions. He urges us to reconcile our
differences, to pluck out offending, infected parts of our
lives, to walk the second mile and turn the other cheek. He
urges us to give the shirts off our backs, to love our enemies, and bless our persecutors with good deeds. He makes
it crystal clear that action is absolutely essential to a disciple.

But then Jesus reminds us that actions triggered by a bad
attitude can be devastating. And that hits all of us, for at
one time or another we have all done the right thing for the
wrong reason. And that is why Christ tells us that the attitudes of our hearts are more important to Him than any
service we render in His name. He calls us to change not
only our ways, but our reasons for doing things as well.

Louie and I have an acquaintance who grew up in a small town where a hard, legalistic attitude prevailed, and anything smacking of feeling and warmth was suspect. In this setting there was a drunk who became the target of much abuse. The "proper" people used him as a bad example to the young: "You don't want to grow up and be like *him,* do you?" But although the unfortunate man's life was in a shambles, he was kind and caring. Our friend sensed this and decided he didn't want to be like the "proper" people: He liked the town drunk better.

Again attitude spoke more clearly than actions.

The Beatitudes are found right in the middle of the Sermon on the Mount. That pleases me. It may not be significant, but for me it is symbolic, for the Beatitudes speak to the core of faith. Right attitudes are the source for good deeds; and in a very real sense, the attitudes we learn and choose to live by determine the kind of persons we become.

To women in particular, in this decade, the Beatitudes carry a special message. We are presented with so many new choices; there are so many more courses of action opening up to us. Wherever we look, we find challenges and opportunities, and we are eager to meet them.

But first there is work to be done within ourselves. A spiritual revolution must take place before our deeds can make a difference in our world. We must learn, from the inside out, what it means to *be* a Christian, to respond to life and our fellow human beings as Christ did, to feel what He felt.

And what better Teacher could we possibly have than the Master Himself! This is what the Beatitudes offer us.

2

How happy are those who know their need for God for the kingdom of Heaven is theirs!

Matthew 5:3

Blessed are the poor in spirit: for theirs is the kingdom of heaven.

Matthew 5:3 KJV

I Can't Make It on My Own, Lord

Poor—I can't imagine anyone *wanting* to be poor; to be totally destitute, in need, anxious, hopeless, frightened. Surely our loving Lord doesn't want this for us?

Yet Jesus says that only if we are poor will we be happy: "Blessed are the poor in spirit: for theirs is the kingdom of heaven" (KJV).

There were many poor people sitting at Jesus' feet when He spoke these words, and He always identified Himself with them. In fact, He told His followers that as they served the "least of these," His brothers and sisters, they would actually be serving Him. But He wasn't telling the poor in the crowd that day that they never had it so good. No, Jesus had great compassion for human need, and the sight of the suffering poor grieved Him. Obviously He was talking about something beyond physical need.

All right, suppose I were in the crowd that came to hear Him speak, and suppose I were poor. I wouldn't have come to get food: He had none. I wouldn't have come for money: He had none. But perhaps I would have come because I needed something else, something that only Jesus could give me.

Yes, now there seems to be new meaning in the word *poor*. I had been thinking in terms of the poverty we're trying to eliminate from our world: hunger, starvation, disease, ignorance. But there is another kind of poverty—devastating, if not as visible. There is a poverty of the spirit. And that's what Jesus is talking about in the first Beatitude.

"Blessed are the poor in *spirit*. . . . " This seems to be the center from which the other Beatitudes radiate. For unless we know how poor we are without Christ, we'll never reach out for Him. If we feel we can take care of ourselves, why ask for help—even from God?

Come to think of it, the happiest people I know are those who have tried and failed—even hit bottom—and then reached out for help. Realizing their spiritual bankruptcy, they asked Jesus to take over their lives. They entered the Kingdom through the door of their own need, and they were met by God's grace.

They're not only the happiest, but the freest people I've known: free to be, to love, and to let God work through them. They enjoy each moment, with no regrets for yesterday and no worries about tomorrow. They don't have to prove anything; they work because they *want* to, not because the world *expects* it of them. To me, these people are very rich—not necessarily in material things, but in the things of the spirit. They possess the peace and joy that come from walking close to God. Yet this route to the Kingdom begins with the painful admission that we are poor and needy. This is the *sine qua non* of our spiritual lives: the most basic fact. We are to trust God, not ourselves, and God means for us to learn that.

For me that learning began during my mid-teens when, without actually seeking it, I had an experience that was both mystical and profound. One evening when I was alone, I went to my room and found myself in the presence of a blinding white light. It was all around me, overwhelming, consuming. I was part of it, and it was part of me. At the core of my being, in my spirit, I felt free and peaceful. I was aware of my oneness with all things, all people, and especially with God.

Since that moment I have never doubted the reality of God or His presence in our human lives. Although that experience wasn't repeated, I still have the strength and assurance it gave me. That was the beginning of my conscious spiritual journey.

For many years I didn't mention that evening to anyone except my mother. In fact, even now I wonder about sharing such an intensely personal incident, for I think we are in trouble when we base our faith upon experience or feeling alone. Yet what we have seen and heard and touched is a valid part of ourselves. For me, that moment was where my pilgrimage began.

In the years that followed I held fast to my faith in God, allowing Him to influence my life but not to guide it; I could do that myself. Then, during my college years, I began to feel a gnawing hunger: There *had* to be more to life than what I saw on the surface. We *had* to do more than go through the motions. There *had* to be meaning, warmth, closeness, love. I was hungry for more of God in my life, but I didn't know where to find Him.

Up to that point my relationship with established religion had been casual. I had wandered in and out of church. Now I looked to the church to show me the way to God. I joined, I worked, I tithed, I tried, and I found only frustration and weariness. The route of "churchianity" was not for me.

By that time I had gone from college to Hollywood, where I was put under contract to a motion-picture studio and promised a creative career. I thoroughly enjoyed my work: It was fun, exciting, and lucrative, and I loved the people! Materially, my background had been very simple, and for the first time in my life I had some of the things I always thought I wanted—plus glamorous surroundings, stimulating work, and talented friends. Yet underneath the surface of my being—deep down in my spirit—my possessions added up to zero. I had more of everything, but "everything" was not enough. The gnawing hunger was still there.

I felt poor—and in a way that had nothing to do with anything external. My poverty was on the inside. True, I had been aware of my spiritual needs for months, but there was always something I could do about them: work harder, try harder, search further. Not anymore. I had run out of things to do. I had done them all, and I was exhausted. And

what good were all my efforts? Where did they get me?
Spiritually I was bankrupt. Let someone else try.

Someone did. At that most needful time in my life I met
a group of young new Christians. They were such warm,
real people, and I felt myself being drawn toward their
loving concern for me. They became my friends, and I
began to hear what they were saying about God.

My friends told me that God was real, but I already knew
that. They said there is a God-sized vacuum in each of us;
and until it is filled with God, we will never have true peace.
I was beginning to know that. But then they told me something I had never known. They told me how to find God!

They said I wouldn't find Him by doing good or by
working harder.

They said I wouldn't find Him through any efforts of my
own.

They said I would find Him through a Person—through
a Person so much like myself that He would understand my
needs, yet Someone so thoroughly *God* that He could feed
my hungry spirit.

At last I understood. At last I had been shown the Way.
My friends urged me to follow it, to give Jesus my impoverished life and let Him make something useful out of it. So
I did. It was quiet and simple, and very, very real. I said yes
to Jesus Christ, and the God I had known to be real—but
far away—came into my life.

What a difference there is between a vague sort of faith
and a personal relationship with a living Christ! He has
given me direction and a goal, and nothing has ever been
quite the same for me. If I had to describe in a few words
how my life has been changed by becoming His disciple, I

would borrow these words from Jesus: ". . . anyone who keeps his life for himself shall lose it; and anyone who loses his life for me shall find it again" (Matthew 16:25 TLB).

Left to ourselves, we find this world a lonely place. No matter how many friends we have or how big our family, we feel cut off from a warmth and love we can't describe. It's always "out there somewhere," until we open our hearts and let the Holy Spirit "in here." He is a part of God Himself, and He will keep us company as long as we live on this earth.

So the spiritual life begins with our becoming poor in spirit. We place our feet on the first step of the ladder and become children of God. Though Matthew never uses the term "new birth," the Beatitudes teach us what it will be like, and they both begin with "I need!"

In our Kingdom-walk we are receivers—doers, too, but receivers first. Yet not all of us accept God's gifts. Some people, because of their pride, cannot reach out and take them. They resent God, and they are never happy.

It is neither wealth nor poverty that keeps us out of the Kingdom. It is our pride that falsely tells us we have no need. Pride lives a very narrow life. It must have all the answers and insists on having its own way. It talks too much. It has trouble getting along with people; it is prejudiced; its ego is so big, you can't help bumping into it. Pride wants too much and offers too little.

Humility is just the opposite: The humble are *not* proud. They know they need help, so they get it. The Kingdom Jesus established is not to be forced on anyone, but gladly given to those who know their need and are ready to receive from God.

Humility is smart enough to know we can't know everything. It listens, and it looks at life through the eyes of others. Humility has many friends because it has time and space in its life for more than itself. The door to its heart is never locked. Humility is thankful for all it has, and because it has received so much, it gives unendingly.

Humility opens the way to God and happiness. Pride stands back, hands at its sides, and says, "No, thanks, I can do it myself." Humility comes with hands outstretched.

Thinking about humility reminds me of two wonderful people we met in Edinburgh many, many years ago. Louie and I had gone to Scotland so that he could complete his graduate studies at New College. We had spent summers in work camps overseas, but this time we were to be away from our country and our family for two years, and we were expecting our first child.

Louie's adviser and New Testament teacher was Professor James Stewart, a man well known as a New Testament scholar and a powerful preacher. We went to hear him preach at Saint George's West on our first Sunday in Edinburgh, and after the service we stayed in our seats for a long time, savoring the inspiration his words had given us. He was a man small in stature and gigantic in spirit—a man of natural talents, disciplined mind, and power uniquely born of the Holy Spirit. We were so grateful that Louie was to learn from this man for the next two years.

As great as he was in the pulpit, Professor Stewart was even more impressive as a human being—and in the gentlest, most humane way. We might have felt homesick those first months had it not been for the many kindnesses he and his lovely wife, Rosamund, sent our way.

They came to see me in the hospital when our son Dan was born six weeks earlier than expected. They invited us to spend Christmas with them and their family, realizing that this was the first time we were away from home for the holidays. And then there were the evenings we and our fellow students spent at their house, drinking Ros's good tea and asking questions of Professor Stewart late into the night. And Ros pedaling over to our flat on her bicycle with flowers picked from her garden, arriving just in time for a "wee visit" while I nursed the "bairn." (We had a baby a year in Scotland, so there was always a bairn.)

The "gift" that meant the most to us came when little Dan was six weeks old. By that time Louie was filling the pulpit in a little country church in Penicuik every Sunday, and we wanted to have our son baptized there. Louie, as Dan's father, couldn't perform the service, and of course you can guess who we wanted to do it. But we just didn't have the nerve to ask.

Getting to Penicuik wasn't easy. It meant a forty-five-minute ride through the Pentland hills—in the middle of winter. A car in postwar Britain was a luxury few of us could afford, so we took a long, bumpy ride on a bus. It was too much to ask—warm and generous as Professor Stewart was, he was still a very busy man. A friend of ours offered to do the service, and we gratefully accepted.

On the morning of Dan's baptism, I dressed him in his warmest and best, and the four of us took the long bus ride to Penicuik. It was cold and the roads were icy, so the ride was longer than usual. When we arrived at the church, I was taken to the vestry. Then, at the appropriate moment in our service, I was led down the aisle, holding Dan in my arms. Out of the corner of my eye I thought I recognized a man sitting in the rear of the church. After the sacrament, I turned to walk back down the aisle, and this time I got a better look. I had been right the first time: It was Professor Stewart! Hearing one of our friends mention that Dan was going to be baptized, he had come all the way out on the bus by himself to be there. After the service he slipped away as quietly as he came. *But he had been there.* In that act, and in countless others like it, he and Ros taught me more about the Christian life and attitude than all his sermons put together. And now these many years later, we have new data that tells us the Stewarts are still giving themselves to others in the same beautiful way. Our youngest son has just returned from studying in Edinburgh, and the highlight of his stay was his friendship with these same two people who walk so humbly with God. (There was however one frustration. Our son James Stewart Evans wanted to learn all he could about his namesake, Professor Stewart, but he could never get him to talk about himself.)

To be poor in spirit is to be in touch with our own need. It's uncomfortable—that's why our spiritual need must be filled before we can touch the needs of others. Before we can appreciate the worth of another human being, we must feel that we ourselves are of value. And many of us don't.

It's a funny thing about pride—often it's a cover-up for a low opinion of the self. It's a way of saying, "All right, world, I know nobody can love me, so I'll look after myself!" It doesn't even give God a chance.

I have a friend, a very lovely person, who, when she was younger, had so little feeling of self-worth that she almost called it quits. She was so desperately in need of self-respect that she was completely unable to give to others. Margot even found it difficult to function as wife and mother, but she covered up her sense of deficiency with a layer of pride. None of us realized how empty she felt inside.

One day Margot felt a mysterious stirring within her. Gently, but persistently, it pushed against her pride until it cracked; without quite understanding what she was doing, Margot reached out for help. She began coming to church for counseling, and when her minister realized how deep her feelings of unworthiness were, he persuaded her to see a sensitive, caring psychiatrist.

It's wonderful how God uses time and people. For many long, tiring months, the minister and the psychiatrist worked with Margot, and through them God was able to bring about a healing in her life.

Margot was driving home from the psychiatrist's office one day after a session that had been a breakthrough—a moment when the light of understanding broke through to her darkened spirit. As she drove through the park she began to feel warmed by that inner light, and suddenly she found herself saying, "Margot, you're a precious person. You're special." Over and over she said it, until she began to cry. She pulled over, stopped the car, and sat basking in a wonderful new awareness of God's love for her.

When Margot started the car to drive home, she did something significant. She reached down and fastened her seat belt. She had never done that before. Now, in one simple action, she was saying, "God cares for me, and *I* care."

Margot was beginning a whole new life that was totally different from anything she had known. Love—God's love —transformed her into a generous and thoughtful person. Being able to receive made her able to give, and as she looked around she saw how much she was needed. At last she could look beyond herself to others.

This past year I experienced a beautiful postscript to this story. On a trip west, Louie and I visited a church where we met person after person who told us how much they had been helped by a gifted, caring psychologist on the church staff. She was a woman with amazing sensitivity to their problems. And, yes—she was Margot.

Christians walk humbly with their Lord, or they don't walk the Way. Humility itself can become proud—proud of being loved, proud of serving, proud of achieving. That's when Jesus reminds us of our poverty—to keep us humble. He takes us through one of life's many Valleys of Humiliation.

I don't know how to avoid these valleys—there are no detours along the Way. And I don't like what I just wrote, but I believe it.

Early in our ministry, Louie and I wanted to go to Africa. Louie had been there as a young man, and he had lost his heart to it. I liked what he told me about the country and especially about the people. In the United States most of us have so many external things, and our hands do not easily reach out to receive what God offers. But in under-developed countries, where people have had to struggle and suffer through disease, famine, and poverty, there seems to be a willingness—even an eagerness—to reach out and accept God's grace.

Hopefully, we offered ourselves—once in the beginning of our ministry and again several years later. Each time the door closed gently but firmly, and finally we got the message: "Keep serving where you are."

And where were we? Right smack in the middle of affluent America!

Don't get me wrong: It's not that I feel a person has to be economically poor to be humble. Some of the most humble people I know are in our present congregation here in Washington, and they would be considered affluent. But material wealth can blind us to the needs of the deprived; exclusive, gracious living can make us forget those who know the gracious life only from movies and TV; built-in security can make us insensitive to those who have to worry about how they will pay their bills all their lives. Worst of all, more than enough can make us forget that we always need Christ.

Gradually Louie and I began to understand the meaning in the door that closed; we have come to see the areas we serve as bursting with potential for God. We are grateful for the challenge and truly humbled by it. But make no mistake about it: There are many Valleys of Humiliation in the City of Affluence. We've been through some of them.

I especially remember when Louie was being installed into the ministry of one of our churches. A minister friend who spent his early life in one of the poorest ghettos of our land was giving the charge to Louie when he pointed a finger at us and said, "I have a feeling that in this place you will have to decrease so that Christ can increase."

They were hard words for us to hear, but our friend was right. In fact, he was prophetic. Through the years Christ has increased; and there have been valleys for us, many of them. But there has also been joy, joy in the fulfilling of the promise that "every valley shall be exalted . . ." (Isaiah 40:4 KJV). It has often been painful for us to be put in touch with our own spiritual need, but it has brought us and kept us close to God. And that *is* happiness!

So, to be poor in spirit is to walk humbly with God. But it is also walking humbly with others.

When we become part of the Kingdom, we join a family, and every other person in the Kingdom becomes our brother or sister. From then on, there can be no conflicting loyalties. The Kingdom is consuming. It is not for the faint-hearted or for those simply "interested in religion," but for those ready to begin a new way of life. Part of this new way is that, unlike the world, the Kingdom is not exclusive. It is for all people without respect to race, color, class, nationality, education, or station in life. As Clarence Jordan said in *The Sermon on the Mount:* "Inside the kingdom there are no partitions. He who would erect them thereby declares himself to be on the outside."

Lord, I don't want to be on the outside. I want to walk humbly with You, my Father, and with all Your other children—my brothers and sisters. Then, and only then, will I be ready to go on to the other Beatitudes.

I need Your gifts so very much, and so I'm going with my hands open and outstretched. I want to learn what it means to be a Christian in the deepest sense. I want to become the kind of person You can use.

Happy is the woman who knows that without God she is nothing, but that with God working through her, she has the strength and power of His love. She has learned the most basic lesson of the spiritual life: to trust God, not herself. Her humility will come from the very center of her being, and it will never allow her to look down on anyone —not even on people who look down on people. And because her humility is real, she will know a bit of heaven right here on earth.

3

Happy are those who know what sorrow means, for
they will be given courage and comfort!

Matthew 5:4

Blessed are they that mourn: for they shall be comforted.

Matthew 5:4 KJV

Lord, I Hurt, and I
Need Your Healing

There was a time when it was hard for me to think about
mourning or to understand how any kind of happiness
could come of it.

Yet in this Beatitude Jesus makes it clear that there is not
only comfort available for the mourner, but joy as well. He
tells us, even urges us, to mourn, to sorrow; so there has
to be something good in it, something beyond the pain.

To *mourn:* What does it mean? "to give way?" "to bend?"
"to break?" Webster says simply, "To feel or express sorrow." That helps a little, and it makes sense. To *mourn* is

to feel pain, to allow it to penetrate us, not to brace our-selves against it. It means we can't pick and choose only the parts of life that we like and reject the rest. No, if we are to experience life truly, deeply, and realistically, we must be vulnerable to all of life, not only its joys, but its sorrows as well.

But there's more, much more, to mourning. Even Web-ster suggests that the feeling of sorrow is not enough. We must express it, let it pass through us. And do we? How often I have heard people say, "Share your joys, but keep your sorrows to yourself." I think I know what they mean —no one likes to be around a person who wallows in self-pity, using sorrow as a means of attracting attention. But that's sickness, not mourning.

The heart was never meant to be a prison for pain. When we stifle an honest expression of real sorrow, we're denying part of our humanity. And if we are Jesus' followers, we're denying His promise: "Happy are those who know what sorrow means, for they will be given courage and comfort!"

The words of this Beatitude are simple, but their implica-tion is deep and sound. It means that there *can* be comfort for our sorrows, but only if we squarely face loss, fear, and anxiety. When we allow ourselves to feel the pain of mourn-ing, then we can be healed. And when Jesus says we will be comforted, it means we will be strengthened and encour-aged. He does not promise that we will be comfortable, but rather, empowered to see it through.

Somehow many of us Christians have come to believe just the opposite. We think that if we become truly spiritual, the blows of life will not reach us; and that if they do, we will have the ability to rise above them instantly. Is this really true? Does Christianity offer some kind of holy immunity against grief and pain? And does "living victoriously" mean living beyond fear, discouragement, loneliness, and desolation? I wonder—I really wonder. If it's true, then the Beatitude is false, and we know it is not.

Jesus is telling us to feel everything. To be spiritually alive is not to be dead to hurt and pain, but to be free to experience them, trusting God to bring us through them safely.

We need the dark nights, sleepless and agonizing as they are. We need the hurts that keep us tender and the unexplained sorrows that stretch our faith and trust. Living through them will make us different people—and the difference can be good!

Many years ago I spent a summer working as a volunteer, helping to build a refugee camp on the outskirts of Paris. I worked side by side with men and women who had been victims of a war, and as we came to know each other as friends their stories gradually tumbled out. They had lived through unbelievable terror and persecution, and although their dark night had passed, the fact that they had suffered would always be a part of their lives. Clearly they were different from the rest of us: Sorrow had taught them what was really important in life. It had made them extremely sensitive to other people's needs. They gave instead of asking; they comforted when others complained. They were some of the most understanding, expressive human beings I have ever met. And through them I learned how God works through our dark nights, using them to deepen the shallow areas of our lives.

Then it's right for Christians to mourn, isn't it, Jesus? Is that what You're telling us in this Beatitude? Are You saying that, as Christians, we should feel more of life, not less? Yes, I think I understand. Unless we open ourselves up to pain and hurt and loss, You cannot heal us; for by shutting out the sorrow, we shut You out, too.

You knew the dark nights, many of them. And when You felt something, You didn't try to hide it. When Your friend Lazarus died, You cried, just the way I cry when a good friend is gone. It's not that I think I won't see my friend again—for I know I will—but I will miss that companionship here on earth.

At National Presbyterian here in Washington, D.C., we are in touch with death thirty or forty times a year. Still I find it hard to accept its frequency and finality. Part of me rejoices, knowing that death opens a door to an existence far more beautiful than I can comprehend. But another part of me—the here-and-now, earthly part—finds it hard to accept the physical separation and the sense of loss. Having known and loved the person within the family of the congregation, I mourn.

When I mourn, I feel pain that seems unbearable at first. But only at first. It doesn't go away quickly—in fact, it doesn't go away at all. It changes. As it pushes back the walls of my resistance to death, the pain itself is softened. Sometimes it turns to tears and sometimes to quiet moments of reflection. It doesn't matter which. The important thing is that I am made vulnerable, receptive—to more pain? Perhaps, but certainly to God's healing love.

But sorrow can be a hardening experience as well. I have a friend who lost someone very close to her, and while many of us tried to comfort her, she wasn't open to a

helping hand, human or divine. Somewhere in her childhood she had been taught to hide her feelings, especially
the sad ones; and today, more than a year after her tragic
loss, she is still unreachable. The pain inside her has grown
in upon itself and become a kind of spiritual malignancy.
The iron will that locks it in, locks the healing out. This
friend is now in the hospital, and I'm concerned about her.
If only she could unlock her heart and let the hurt, the
loneliness, and the bitterness out into the open where Jesus
could apply His healing light. If only she could believe that
God can mend any broken heart when He is given all the
pieces. Then perhaps she could share her grief with a
friend; for God uses people in His healing process, too, and
there are many who care. I pray she will—oh, how I pray
she will! But the decision is hers. The lock on the door of
my friend's heart is on the inside, and only she can open
it.

How different the experience of mourning has been in
the life of another good friend. Mary and Joel were two of
the most beautiful people I've ever known. They met and
married a little later than most couples and were blessed
with an immense capacity to enjoy each other. I knew them
through my work when I was a single career girl, and I don't
think they ever realized how much inspiration I found just
being in their home. Joel was quite a powerful man in our
field, but he was even more impressive as a human being:
so warm, open, communicative, and real. His wife, Mary,
was a vivacious, outgoing woman who deserved him in
every way. In an industry not known for happy marriages,
theirs was an uncommonly good one.

For many years Mary and Joel were childless. Then Mary

gave birth to a son who brought new meaning and joy to their very happy home. Suddenly it was over. There wasn't even a warning. One day Joel had a heart attack, and a few hours later he was gone. Everybody who knew and loved him was shocked, but Mary's loss seemed unbearable. She was a strong-minded person who always seemed able to face anything in life, but could she face death?

I was with Mary soon after Joel died, and I'll never forget what she said: "Oh, Colleen, life will never be the same without him." I wondered whether she would be able to go on with life at all. How I longed to share her suffering, to bring some rest to the tired, sleepless eyes. But I could only wait, and pray, and hope.

I couldn't help asking myself whether Joel's death would have been more bearable if Mary had been prepared for it —perhaps a lingering illness softens the final blow? But as I and Mary's other friends watched her go through her dark night, we realized that death—whenever it comes, however it comes—is a stunning, rending loss.

Death will come to all of us and to all we know and love. Yet it's only a word, never real, until it strikes close to us. There is nothing we can do beforehand to lessen its pain. It will pass through us or remain forever outside us waiting to get in. It will not go away.

Mourning may seem to be a cruel season, but God doesn't bring it upon us as a punishment or a toughening process. Mourning is part of our human condition. Because we can love, and because we need love, we must get close to other human beings. Our lives touch and mingle; we add to each other; and when a loved one is torn away, our love bleeds. That is mourning.

If there were some preventive spiritual medicine we could take ahead of time to lessen the pain and shorten the long days and weeks and months of sorrow, what then? Mourning would be simply an event that occurred, an obstacle along our way, but nothing that left its mark upon us. No happiness could possibly come of it, for we would never reach the second part of the Beatitude—God's refining, deepening, life-changing comfort.

I understood that when I watched Mary struggle with her pain. Gradually the confusion began to sort itself out, and she felt some of her former strength returning. She had been right: Life *wouldn't* be the same for her without Joel. Not ever. But God, working through the love and warmth of Mary's friends, helped her to see that life was still good. That appreciation was something she wanted to pass on to her son. And she did. Because she left herself open to sorrow, yet never indulged herself in it, she found Someone to share it with her. Then, when she was strong enough, she was able to help lift the burden of grief from her child.

Fern, another very special friend of mine, was a different kind of woman. Quiet, soft-spoken, vulnerable, her whole existence revolved around her young doctor-husband. They were happy; they had much to look forward to—and then Tom was gone and there was nothing left. Or so it seemed to Fern. Later she told me about those terrible days.

At first there was shock, a refusal to believe that Tom was dead. Then there was contempt for the life that lay ahead of her, a life she didn't want to live. For besides Fern's loneliness, there were practical problems to face: two children to support, her husband's aging mother to care for, very little money, no job and no training for one.

Even worse was the call from the tomb, the visits to the graveside again and again. "I was like the women who went to Christ's tomb, weeping and carrying spices, expecting to minister to His body," Fern said. "But you remember how the angel met them at the tomb and told them that Jesus wasn't there? In a way, that's what happened to me. One day I began to cry, and that was the beginning of my letting go of sorrow. I could feel God standing close to me, and I knew that my tears were part of His therapy. He came to me through them, because then He could get at my pain."

Fern realized that she had to make a decision. If she truly believed in God's promise of comfort, she had to trust Him completely. She had to depend on Him to give her the courage to face life again. Of course she couldn't do it herself, and that's why the future had looked so impossibly difficult to her. She never could have found her way alone in such darkness. But she didn't have to. There was a Light, and oh, what an eager receiver she was! She not only accepted the Light, she absorbed it. It became part of her.

"God brings us comfort in so many ways," Fern said. "I could see Him reaching out to heal me through other people—in a handshake, in a smile, or a single word. And then one day, after another sleepless night, I saw Him in the sunrise; and I realized then that I had forgotten that the sun *does* rise every day. I had been looking only at the sunsets.

"At last I could commit Tom to God and stop being a tomb looker. I knew that eventually I would be able to feel joy because my husband was in the presence of the Risen Lord. It was as if the stone of sorrow, like the stone closing

Christ's tomb, had been rolled aside, and I could see that God was there.''

It was time for Fern to go on in life. We all knew it because we could feel God working through us to help her. First there was a job—a job she could handle and one that gave her room to grow. Then there were friends and family to help care for the children and Tom's mother, giving Fern time to adjust to the demands of a home and a job. Finally there was joy—joy in her memories of a wonderful life with Tom, recalling the happy times they shared, the struggles that brought them closer and deepened their lives. Then anticipation of the reunion they would have someday.

Fern never pitied herself, never became morbid on holidays or on the anniversary of Tom's death. "God wants us to celebrate life," she said. "And Tom isn't dead."

Neither is Fern. There is a lot of life for her to live. And she has become strong. In fact, she has become a great blessing to others in their mourning by helping many to turn away from the tomb. How often I have heard that Fern has helped some mutual friend turn the corner—going with that person to the graveside, helping to pray these simple, healing words:

Oh, God, let this sorrow that has come upon me be to Your Glory,
and reveal Yourself to others through it.
I accept it, Lord. Let Your name be glorified through it.

Fern came through her dark night because she opened herself up to its pain. She mourned as deeply as anyone I have ever known, and she was comforted by a loving God. She has truly lived this Beatitude, and I have seen happiness, hers and others, come out of sorrow.

As I began this chapter, I said there was a time in my life when I found it almost impossible to understand how any kind of joy could be part of the mourning experience. But that time is no more.

In recent years I have experienced this joy for myself, and I know it to be real. I still feel tender when I think of the night Louie and I were wakened from a deep sleep by the ringing of the telephone. I jumped out of bed and reached for the phone on my desk.

It was a long-distance call for me from my stepfather in California. His voice was full of anguish.

"Oh, my God, I can't believe it. My Stella's gone. Your mother's dead."

Mother gone? She couldn't be! I had talked to her the day before. I knew she had not been feeling well and was having tests. But gone? No, God, no!

"Heart attack," he said.

I felt a cold mass in my chest, and I began to tremble.

"Jim, just hold on. I'll be there with you just as soon as I can get a flight out."

I was aware of his awful need and wanted to comfort him, but my own pain and loss were overwhelming me.

I fell to my knees beside our bed. Waves of sorrow washed over me as I thought of the woman who had been both mother and father to me as I grew up, the one who so committed herself to me that I always felt secure in her love and safe in the home she worked so hard to maintain. She had always been such a pal—so much fun—a terrific mother. Even after my marriage, though miles and long stretches of time separated us, we remained close.

I ached to hold her or walk with her hand in mine as we had always done when we were together. My sorrow and shock were too deep for tears. Everything in me cried out, "God, help! I can't make it without You."

I didn't know what to ask Him for; I could only abandon myself to His strength to fill my weakness.

As I knelt there, calling, crying to God, I was aware of a change gently coming over me. A warm blanket of love enveloped me. I felt His strength absorb my weakness. The pain was still there, but somehow I knew I would not only make it, but there would be strength to share with others.

On the flight to California my mourning began, and the much needed tears began to flow. Even in the midst of them I marveled that my heart could hurt so much and yet I could feel such all-pervading peace.

The powerful, comforting presence of God was with me in the days that followed as I went about doing the work of death. I was qualitatively stronger than my usual self, and I knew it was a work of God. Leaning on Him every moment, asking and receiving what He gave, I experienced His power and peace as a fruit of His Spirit in me. It continued, and I knew firsthand that the comfort of the Holy Spirit in our times of mourning is real.

The reality of the Spirit's comfort in mourning does not make us immune to tender moments and pain. The Holy Spirit does not make us feel less, but enables us to handle more.

My mother-in-law, Marie Evans, recently said good-bye to her lifelong companion. When my husband's father, Dr.

Louis Evans, Sr., died, we in the family witnessed the pure beauty of a life submitted as we watched Marie walk through those days. The power of the Holy Spirit in her life gave us all permission to celebrate daddy's long life and fruitful ministry as Christians should.

However, there are moments, and Marie acknowledges them openly. She shared with me some perceptive thoughts she received in a note from a near-ninety-year-old friend:

Dear Marie,

Now the "Spiritual Adrenalin" that pours into our days of crisis has passed and you are beginning to reorganize your entire life. This terrible freedom from 60 years of uninterrupted concern and activity for and with the Beloved.

There seemed to me an insoluble inner conflict in dealing with the immense pile of demands for every ounce of energy, and an emptiness that made it seem as if nothing mattered. I think you will handle all this magnificently.

The unexpected little things seemed hardest: a half-finished letter, a sock that doesn't match—a spoon misplaced—or a sudden memory.

"We rejoice for him . . . it is ourselves for whom we mourn." These two are one, by the grace of God. This is our faith. But the quick smile—touch—exchange of glances—and our defenses are down.

Death is not the only human experience that ushers mourning into our lives. In the summer, when our family goes traveling, we often contact old friends—some from college or seminary days, some from previous pastorates, and some I worked with years ago. It's wonderful to see them, and within a few short hours we always manage to catch up on the years of living. That's the way it is with good friends.

We're happy when we find our friends growing, stretching, and enjoying God's good life, and we celebrate with them. But sometimes we come upon friends in mourning, and it's not always death that lays them low. One friend may mourn a marriage broken after twenty-five years. Another mourns for an adult daughter stubbornly pursuing a course of life that will ultimately hurt her and others. Another is recovering from a mastectomy and realistically facing what this means to a woman. She mourns over the physical, emotional, and psychological shock to the core of her femininity.

As our friends honestly expose their pain to us and to God, as they open up and become vulnerable to Him, His light and love begin to do what only they can do: They heal. We have seen it happen, even in the midst of pain. As one friend said, "It hurts like crazy, but I'm beginning to feel this unexplainable peace. It has to be from God." And of course it is.

Very often there is nothing we can do beyond mourning. We must wait for comfort and the strength to go on. But there are other times when mourning is only the beginning of something that must be done. A mourner is not always one who weeps, but one who expresses sorrow, or concern. Tears are not essential to mourning, but genuine concern is—concern that ends in action.

I'm thinking of You, Jesus, when You mourned for the city of Jerusalem. You wept as You opened Yourself up to its agony, and then You went into the city to teach, to preach, and to heal. You did something about the causes of suffering.

Why do I find this kind of mourning so difficult, Lord? I'm learning to give myself up to a personal loss or tragedy, but this is something else. It's not always enough for me to feel someone else's pain, is it? And I can't express it simply in words or the touch of a hand. Much more is needed. In fact, this kind of mourning is very expensive: It means I must act. I must go to Jerusalem.

Perhaps, sensing the cost, I unconsciously try to shield myself. I turn away from this "Jerusalem" kind of mourning. Yes, a lot of us do. But You understand, Jesus, and You find ways to jolt us out of our apathy and bring us up close to our suffering, hurting, fellow human beings.

I'm remembering when our family lived in La Jolla some years ago and we became interested in a project our church was involved in just across the border in Mexico. Along with several other churches and civic groups, we were helping to maintain a day school and maternity clinic in an impoverished area. Louie and I wanted to see how the project was coming along, so we asked the young minister in charge of it if our family could tag along on his next trip across the border. He agreed, and one beautiful, sunny Saturday morning the six of us piled into our car and followed our friend south for forty-five minutes. We were in another world.

We drove around a town bustling with tourists and shoppers and made our way to the hills and canyons. There, surrounded by hundreds of tiny shacks made of packing crates, scraps of tin, and cardboard boxes, was the Casa—day school, maternity clinic, and chapel, all in one small area.

I had spent summers in work camps; I had seen the aftermath of war; I was no stranger to deprivation. But I was not prepared for what I saw in those grim hills. This was poverty, and I will never use the word casually again.

I hope I'll always remember that day in my life. It's hard to believe that hope can rise from such depression, yet it did. Hope came in the form of the people who kept the Casa going: the lovely old Mexican lady who first saw the need for help many years ago and whose very presence had been an inspiration to the staff, the Mexican teacher who ran the school, the American doctor who worked there one day a week on her own time, and the volunteers who prepared and served the children the only food most of them would eat all day. Truly, they were doers of the Word.

Children are quick to make friends, and as our four played with the Casa schoolchildren we talked as well as we could with the staff. There was a language barrier because none of us spoke fluent Spanish and the Mexicans spoke very little English, but we found that our hands and eyes could say a lot for us.

It was a long, quiet drive home that evening. No one—not even Jamie, our youngest and liveliest who was then a very young child—had much to say. When we arrived at our home (which suddenly looked very grand) we each went our own way, lost in our private thoughts. There was little sleep for any of us that night. We were in mourning.

We woke up feeling restless. We had wept for Jerusalem, and now we wanted to do something—personally—about the misery we had seen there. But what?

Dan, our oldest son, was about eleven when we took our first trip to the Casa. Thoughtful, frugal with words, he didn't say much about how he felt. But at Christmastime that year, something he did told us very clearly. The students in his school decided not to exchange gifts with each other. Instead they sent food and toys to the Casa. The idea was Dan's, as we learned later from his principal. As head of the student council he had suggested the plan at a meeting, and when it was approved, he helped organize it. Our son went to Jerusalem.

A few years later, during Easter vacation, Dan visited the Casa again. This time he went with a lot of his friends from church, and they spent their vacation painting and repairing the school. It was a rewarding time for all of them.

Dan's ability to mourn, to feel another person's sorrow, has become an important part of his life. More and more we see it shaping him, leading him in ways that are right for him. He is now in law school, and working for a congressman—dealing with issues of justice and human rights. He is a concerned young man who feels his life is in some way meant to make a difference for the "least of these," Christ's brothers and sisters. He does it quietly, simply, as a way of making his faith credible.

We're not all like Dan. Some of us take different roads to Jerusalem. Some of us turn back. It all depends upon our ability to sense sorrow and injustice and our will to do something about them.

For some reason it helps me to experience sorrow directly or to know personally someone who is being mis-treated—then I am stirred into action. It's just the way I am, the road I have to take.

One day many years ago (in fact, so many years that Jamie—then a lively third grader—is now a senior in col-lege) I had a call from the mother of one of Jamie's class-mates. Her name is Amy. She told me that the third grade, an unusually large class, was desperate for a room mother. Amy had been asked to help out, and she said she would if another mother would share the load. I knew what was coming: Would I be that other mother?

Well, I had just decided that my basket was full enough for the coming year. So I took a deep breath and explained how busy I was with children going to different schools, my church work, and a few community activities. I saved the clincher for last: "You see, we have *four* children."

"Yes, I know," she said. "We have seven."

Well, I became Amy's helper for the year. We gave class parties and organized the usual activities during the holi-days—and it was fun! We were a good team, and I made a wonderful new friend. Amy was a warm, open, consid-erate woman with a delightful sense of humor. We under-stood each other and could share the way we felt about our faith, our families, and the plain joy of being alive. It was a treat for us to be together. One night we even suc-ceeded in getting our busy husbands to take us to a foot-ball game.

Then something happened to change my relationship with Amy—and my life as well. I had a dream one night, and I, who can rarely remember my dreams, can still *feel* this one. In my dream I became Amy, and her children were mine. We were living in tiny rooms so crowded and cluttered that I felt I was losing my sense of dignity as a human being.

I woke up the next morning, a Sunday, feeling uneasy, angry, almost ill. I knew I had to find Amy, and when I went to church she was there, looking for me. For the first time since I had known her, the smile was gone from her face and her eyes were filled with tears. Would we be home that afternoon? She needed to talk.

We talked. That afternoon Louie and I discovered another woman beneath Amy's cheerful, bouncy exterior. For Amy is black, and that day she told us what her life was really like—overworked, underpaid, she and her husband and the children jammed into a four-room apartment because that was all they could afford.

This is important: Amy wasn't bitter. She didn't feel sorry for herself. She didn't think the world owed her anything. But she was a woman, a wife, a mother, and she was hurting for her family. Oh, how she was hurting!

Knowing Amy, loving her as a friend, we hurt with her. We mourned, and we wanted to help. How?

Somewhere in my memory something was calling for attention. What was it? A project—something our church mission commission was doing, something that had caught my mind and interest, but not my heart.

I remembered! As I listened to Amy that Sunday and saw the pain in her eyes, I remembered that our mission commission had talked about sponsoring a low-income housing project for minority groups. A study had convinced them that this was our community's most urgent need. I knew the project was still in the works, but my passive support had not been enough to keep me informed of where it was at the moment.

Now it was different. I had a personal stake in that housing development because I was learning what it was like to live without it. And I knew what it would mean to someone I loved. Multiply that feeling by the number of families who could live in those new houses, and you have a project that finally gets under way. Somehow two churches got together. Somehow two official boards joined forces under a determined and dedicated black pastor and our minister of missions. Somehow our congregations began to feel what I had felt: human need—not somebody else's need, but our own, for we were all one. I looked at an architect's drawing of the project. Here and there in the split-level buildings the architect had sketched little stick figures representing men and women. But that wasn't what I really saw. No. I saw my friend Amy and her wonderful family comfortably settled in one of the larger apartments. And through seeing them, I saw their neighbors—*my* neighbors.

Now that we live in the inner city of the District of Columbia, I am again finding that I am most deeply stirred by relationships. Though I serve on a board that sees to urban needs and am a member of a hunger committee, it is the people I see from day to day—my neighbors in need—who most touch my heart. The figures and statistics we work with at board meetings are important, but it is the faces I cannot forget.

The other day the bells of the church across the square from where we live were ringing as they do every noon. The tune was familiar: "God will take care of you." As I whispered the words to the melody I looked out the window to the square below. There on the bench just a few yards from our front door was a young man, sleeping. He carries a bag of belongings; I have seen him many times. We are not yet friends, only acquaintances, but I know his name is Gene; he has been looking for work, and he is the age of our youngest son. Perhaps in time Louie and I can build a relationship of trust with Gene. Perhaps we can meet with our friend who has been used by God in finding jobs for the difficult to employ—but then again, perhaps not. But we will try, for the chimes ring the truth. God does want to take care of His children—all of them—and part of His plan for accomplishing this is to teach *us* to care for one another.

Thank You, Lord, for Gene, for Amy, and for all the others you will put in my life. I need them. I want to be able to mourn, not only for myself but for others, just as You did. I want to be able to sense human need, and with Your help to find a way to meet that need. But first I must be free —free to feel sorrow. I'm not afraid of it anymore, for I, too, have seen the sun rise after the dark night. And it always will.

Happy is the woman who honestly faces her loss and opens herself up to sorrow in her life and in her world. Because she trusts God to come to her and heal her wounded spirit, she finds a new and deeper meaning in His presence. She knows that she will never again be the same woman, but she also knows that she is not alone. He is there in the loving gestures of the friends who walk close beside her; He is there to take over when she is helpless to help herself. His strength becomes hers, as in her weakness she abandons herself to Him. Happy is the woman who mourns, for God is able to be her comfort and her strength.

4

Happy are those who claim nothing, for the whole earth will belong to them!

Matthew 5:5

Blessed are the meek: for they shall inherit the earth.

Matthew 5:5 KJV

Lord, Give Me Gentle-Power

I have a problem with this Beatitude. Frankly, I've never cared for it. Usually I pass over it quickly and try to ignore it.

The word *meekness* bothers me. When I think of someone meek, I see a mousy, Caspar Milquetoast type of person, and I react. In fact, I react so strongly that when I come to the words "Gentle Jesus, meek and mild," I want to stop singing the hymn. That isn't the way I see Jesus. I see Him strong—gentle, yes, but certainly not meek.

Still, I can't accept all the other Beatitudes, with their

revolutionary effects on my life and pretend this one isn't
there. Jesus apparently thought it was important. He included it among the most practical guidelines Christians
have ever been given. I must find out why. Apparently I
have misunderstood it.

Perhaps the word *meekness* meant something different
when Jesus used it. I've never taken the time to learn the
original languages in which the Bible was written. I'll have
to read what scholars have to say. They can help me understand the historical background. I need to sense the setting
in which the word was used. As I ask the Holy Spirit to teach
me, He often leads me to the work of a scholar—one whose
gift opens up a wide new area of meaning to me.

I have looked up the word *meekness* in the dictionary, but
it appears we have no single word to describe what *meekness*
means in the biblical sense. So I go to my Bible. As I search
its pages, some new meaning begins to appear. In the Bible
meek is used to describe two men—Moses and Jesus—which
says a lot in itself.

Moses, Prince of God, who stood against the might of
Egypt (Numbers 12:3), and Jesus, who defied the power of
Rome (Matthew 11:29)—neither could be considered weak
or fearful. So what about meekness? What does it mean?
Ah, here it comes: A meek person doesn't fight or argue
with God. He doesn't defy His ways. No, just the opposite.
A meek person submits his will to God. He trusts God to
shape his will into a force for goodness, into something
God can use.

As I pondered this deeper meaning, mumbling to myself,
my husband's curiosity was aroused. He pulled his Greek
New Testament from the shelf and read Matthew 5 aloud.

Then he checked it against his lexicon, and suddenly we both became excited about the new ideas that became apparent.

The Greek word for meek is *praus.* When used to describe sound, it means "soft and gentle." When used to describe an animal, it means "a wild animal that has been tamed": one no less strong, but one whose strength has been channeled and made usable.

And when *praus* is used to describe a human being, it refers to a person who has been gentled, quieted, particularly after anger. This is not a weak person. This is a strong, spirited individual who has been tamed—molded—by God. He no longer flies off in all directions; he has a Way to go. Neither is his spirit broken. With God working through it, it is stronger than ever.

Meekness, then, means "strength," but not raw power that may strike out and destroy. Meekness is gentle-power. It builds, it lifts up, it restores.

The meek are the submitted ones. They have surrendered their human wills to God so that He can use them as instruments of His power on this earth.

As I continue to research this word that is growing in interest, I see that in the early church the submitted people were not doormats. In fact, they were called "the terrible meek," for they were fearless with anyone who tried to make them compromise or disobey the Master. (Acts 5:29: ". . . It is our duty to obey the orders of God rather than the orders of men.") It occurs to me that this is the stuff of which martyrs are made, and the church throughout history has been made stronger through their meekness.

In a personal vein, the combination of submission with

strength reminds me of two men we know who have similar qualities but use them in totally different ways. They both have talent, strong egos, and fascinating personalities, but that's where the similarity ends. One man lives for himself, driven by an ambition that can't seem to be satisfied. It isn't that he is cruel to his family or that he doesn't care about them. I think he cares very much. But he seems to be driven, both in his career as head of a large corporation and in his social life among VIPs who are always arriving, departing, overlapping. He is also driven in his personal life. I get the feeling that he never wants to be alone, that perhaps he's afraid to be. But periodically his doctor puts him in the hospital for a few weeks, with a strictly enforced NO VISITORS sign on his door. And he is alone, but not by choice.

I don't know what drives our friend. It could be his desire for money, power, and position; or it could be some missing link in the chain of his life that makes him feel he has to prove something in order to be accepted by himself and the world. At any rate, I don't have to know why, because there is Someone who knows everything about our friend and He is the only One who can change his life patterns.

Louie and I care about this man, and we pray that one day he will submit his life, with all its drivenness, to the One who knows and cares and can do something to help.

The other man, equally aggressive and magnetic, has submitted his life to Christ, and what a difference that has made! Now, instead of using people, he allows God to use him as a blessing to so many lives.

He wasn't always that way. Louie and I met him before he knew Christ, and while he was an attractive person, there was something reckless, almost self-destructive about him.

We met him at one of the few parties Louie and I have time to attend. I guess it's because I love people that I enjoy a good party. It's an adventure! There's always someone new to meet, someone whose life may be meant to touch mine, someone to be used by God to teach me something, and hopefully it works the other way around. That's why, before I go to a party, I pray that I will be drawn toward the person God wants. And it has happened—many times.

It happened the night we met Hal. Just before we all sat down to dinner, there was a commotion at the door. There was a late and very noisy guest arriving. It was Hal. Obviously this wasn't his first party of the evening. Or perhaps he had had one all by himself before leaving home. Still, he was ready for conversation—in fact, he dominated it.

It was amazing how this man's presence seemed to fill the room. No doubt about it: Here was a compelling, powerful personality. On the surface he was rough and loud, but as Louie and I were seated next to him for the rest of the evening, we began to see that the real man, the man underneath the scratchy surface, had great warmth, love, and sensitivity. We couldn't help thinking of the wonderful things God could do through such a man, if only—but Hal by his own admission was not a believer. He didn't seem to believe in anything but himself. Much as we coveted him for the Lord, we could only pray and wait.

Then, one Sunday a few weeks later, Hal and his whole family came to church—for the first time! I'm not sure why —perhaps out of curiosity, maybe a feeling of need. Anyway, it was just the beginning. In the months that followed,

Hal stopped running his own life and turned it over to Christ.

Of course, I'm oversimplifying; it didn't happen that quickly. Nor did Hal give in easily. He struggled against submitting that powerful will to God, and at times he still struggles. From friends who knew him during his pre-Christian days, we learned that he was a man given to extremes. Some of this tendency remains. We see it cropping up every now and then, when he tries to manipulate people into experiencing their faith in "the right way" (*his* way), when he tried to link faith in Christ with a narrow political position. But always, because he is sincere in his commitment to Christ and puts Him before his own interests, he abandons these tactics. He allows himself to be led to where Christ is central to everything else in life. It's almost as if God had whispered to him, "You may be extreme in your love for Me, and in your love for your brothers and sisters in life, but nowhere else!"

Yes, Hal still struggles—but God wins. Now the real Hal has come to the surface, where everyone can see him. He's a wonderful worker—not only in the church, but out in the community, where his dynamic talents can do so much good. There seems to be no end to the things he can accomplish, but there is a difference in the way he uses his abilities. His strength—as great as ever—has been tamed. He uses it to lift up rather than to crush. Hal has gentle-power.

Perhaps we must be strong before we can be gentle. It's a matter of learning how to use our muscles, spiritual as well as physical: the hand that strikes, learning to shield; the tongue that wounds, learning words of comfort; seeking out a person's needs so that we may help instead of attack.

Yes, I'm beginning to like this word *meekness.* And I wonder if it stretches the meaning too far to think of a meek person as someone bendable, adaptable to God and to life. I think it fits, and I think I need more meekness in my own life. So many things are changing today: our way of life, our values, our children, our institutions. I want to be able to shift gears easily, to understand and appreciate what is going on around me, to be strong in holding fast to what is important and adaptable in letting go of that which is not. So I can't be rigid. I must be bendable, strong enough on the inside to adapt on the outside. In other words, I must be meek in order to meet tomorrow.

Adaptable: That's a word I really like. Happy are the adaptable. It makes a lot of sense in our world. The unhappy people are the ones who feel threatened by the changes going on around them. They have little inner strength, so they look to traditions and institutions to give them a sense of security. Newness frightens them; they become rigid, and in their presence there is no peace.

But there are others who haven't hardened. Feeling the flow of life, they move in rhythm with it. Their trust in Christ is so real, and the security He gives them is so strong, that they cannot be threatened by change. They realize that newness is inherent in life, and if they are going to expand and grow, they too must change. But they aren't dominated by change—they are free to evaluate it, to reject or accept it, according to its merits. These are the meek people of the world; and when I am with them, I sense peace. With God's help, I want to be more like them. Meek people don't make a lot of noise about their rights. They will work for the rights of others, and in doing so they secure rights for all, themselves included. As Dr. Ralph Sockman stressed in *The Higher Happiness,* the meek are more concerned with their responsibilities. Instead of grabbing, they offer. While others fight their way through life, the meek walk quietly about, getting things done. They are concerned more with justice for all than with justifying themselves.

Yes, I can envision these people inheriting the earth, not by seizing it with force. The earth will come to them as a gift, because they are the true children of God.

I need to be adaptable. It's not only my world that is changing: My home is, too—constantly. The only sure thing about my schedule for any given day is that it will change.

During the past few years, since I have been working, Louie and I have reached a new level of adaptability in our marriage.

For example, my calendar reminds me that this coming week we are to host the church Pastoral Services Committee for lunch one day, the new members for a dessert that same night, and a group of young singles for a fellowship dinner another evening. My "Month at a Glance" also tells me I have a writing deadline to meet by the end of the week. Obviously there is no way I will get everything accomplished without Louie's cooperation and adaptability. And fortunately for me, I will have them.

This is a new season for us, and it has brought some changes in the way we live and do things. The most obvious change is that Louie has released me from the care of a too-large (for *this* season) house and yard to a much simpler, more convenient situation in the city. While he loved the open spaces and seclusion of suburbia, he has not only adapted to our new home but has become an enthusiastic convert to our simpler life. Actually it has freed us both.

He has also cut back significantly in his requests to hold meetings in our home. Three groups in one week may not seem like it, but that is about half what we used to average in the same amount of time. We both love offering hospitality, but we found I could not keep my writing commitments when I was also being hostess to the whole world. Louie has adjusted his desires in order to help me be accountable in my work. I appreciate that.

I also appreciate it when he sees I am in a bind and makes an effort to help with some of the chores. Now he will often go with me to the market, where we divide the grocery list and get the shopping done in half the time. When we come home, he helps me lug in the heavy jugs of cider I mull all winter long for church gatherings, and he helps put away the groceries like an efficiency expert.

If I have been writing all day and have totally forgotten (and I *can* totally forget!) we are expecting company, he pitches in to help make the house presentable.

Early in our marriage, it would have been difficult for me to ask for this kind of help from Louie. What I see our daughter and son-in-law and other young couples doing so naturally today would not have been natural for me—then. But then was then, and now is now. We are in a new season, and Louie's willingness to adapt is making it a very meaningful one.

I also am learning to reduce the expectations and demands I make of myself. I love to cook, but have to accept the fact that when I am on a writing deadline and working all day, I cannot expect to serve gourmet meals at night. I have learned to take shortcuts, and my family has adapted without complaint (most of the time!).

With so many women working outside the home today, I think it is important to realize that husbands and wives now work together to provide a warm, hospitable base for family and friends. We may have to learn to take shortcuts at times and to accept help with the chores from other family members. But the attitude of a family is what really counts, and when love and warmth and welcome prevail, the shortcuts will scarcely be noticed.

Adaptability is something I've had to learn over the years, and I think God has used the circumstances of my life to make me more flexible. During the early years of our marriage I wanted so much to please, but it was hard for me to adjust to unexpected guests and interrupted plans for the day. I was used to an ordered, methodical way of life, and suddenly my days were crowded with spontaneous activity. What a good thing it is that God created us with a built-in ability to change.

When I married Louie, one of my friends said I married into a family that crowds more into a week than most families do in a year. And she was right. It was like jumping onto a fast-moving train! It was fun, and I loved my new family —but sometimes I had to hold on for dear life! The truth is, they had a lot to teach me about being adaptable— especially my mother-in-law, who to me will always be the Queen of Adaptability.

Even during our student years, we didn't just go to school—we traveled for the seminary and worked with young people. Later, studying in Scotland, we served a country church part-time. Now I can look back with gratitude for the experience.

I remember when we took our first full-time position in a church and found ourselves deeply involved in the lives of many people; it was a whole new world of sharing, giving, and caring. I had never known such happiness. I had also never known such busyness. The last shreds of my ordered, methodical existence were fraying rapidly. I could feel myself becoming rigid, resisting the changes going on in my life. Then I realized that *I* would also have to change. I would be rigid and sink or become flexible and learn to swim. I couldn't change overnight: We human beings aren't made that way. But I knew, too, that God would help me to adapt, little by little. And of course He did.

Now interruptions are so much a part of my life that I can hardly believe I ever resented them. Surprisingly, I have found "swimming" stimulating and pleasant, so long as I have a little raft in the sun where I can climb aboard and be totally alone. I'm talking about the time I set aside for myself every day, no matter how hectic life may be. This is my time: my time for prayer, for books, for quietness, or simply goofing off. It is the one ordered part of my life, and when my own inner needs have been met, I find that I am much more adaptable to the needs of the people around me. It seems that in taming us, God makes us useful to the others in our lives.

Meekness. It's beginning to sound better, stronger, now that I know more about it. And meekness is something I need every day, for I must be adaptable to far more than the changes that occur in my world. I must develop an attitude of meekness—of adaptability—to the people around me, especially my family. For those of us who are married, this means our spouses, first of all.

I'm well aware that in these days we react uncomfortably to the very word *submission,* but I think this is because we misunderstand what Paul is saying to the Ephesian Christians, and to us, in Ephesians 5. We take the verse "wives, be subject to your husbands, as to the Lord" (RSV) and forget that this section on Christian marriage begins with the apostle calling for a mutual giving of husbands and wives: "Be subject to one another out of reverence for Christ" (RSV). To me this says a marriage honors Christ as both partners submit themselves to each other. As I think about the couples we know, the greatest marriages among them work along these lines. The presupposition is that two whole people—redeemed, healed, growing partners—are subject to the Lord, and to each other as Christians.

If Christ is our model, then our mutual submission to each other will never suppress or violate what is strongest and best in each of us. Nor will it ever violate the Spirit of His gospel. Christ's lordship over His people—both husbands and wives—would never allow them to be subject to anything unhealthy or degrading in a relationship. Nor is submission synonymous with being a doormat. It means giving as opposed to being used. It involves a beautiful reciprocity.

This is not to say there won't be times when circumstances or need asks more of one partner or the other. But over the long span of years there will be a balance that will

leave both husband and wife feeling cherished and satisfied. Or so I think it is meant to be—and can be!

Submission is not a word for women only. It is for Christians, male and female. When we submit to one another out
of reverence for Christ, we are not making doormats of
ourselves; we are simply being obedient.

Paul says that husbands are to express their mutual submission and "headship" by loving their wives: "as Christ
loved the church and gave himself up for her" and ". . . as
[they love] their own bodies. . ." (RSV).

Louie and I have some very special friends here in Washington. Mary Jane and John Dellenback have been such
models to us—and to many others—in their support of
each other's dreams.

For many years John was in politics, and Mary Jane could
not have been more supportive in her role as his wife.
There is so much I could say about her effectiveness on his
behalf. She believed in him and what he was doing so
thoroughly that she became a powerful asset to his career.
They were a team in the true sense.

Then John shifted from elected public office to another
form of public service that was a great challenge for him,
but did not call for as much of Mary Jane's active participa-
tion. At that point she began to dream a dream of her
own.

One day Mary Jane walked into Louie's office at church
and began to share her hopes with him.

"Louie, I'd like to finish my undergraduate degree, then
go on to prepare myself for a career in counseling."

"What then?" Louie asked.

"Then I'd like to counsel," she replied.

"Where would you like to do that, in what sort of sur-roundings?"

"Here at National Church," was her immediate answer. "I'd like to set up a counseling center." Louie said her eyes were twinkling with excitement.

Mary Jane's husband had just finished an important government assignment. He had thought of returning to the West Coast to manage some business holdings he had there, but after talking with Mary Jane, he decided to submit to her dream. He found a job in Washington and became what he called a "sojourner" so that he could support his wife in the realization of her God-given desire.

Louie and I were deeply impressed with John's love. Here was a man willing to give up something of himself, just as ". . . Christ loved the church and gave himself up for her" (RSV). For several years he cheerfully undergirded his wife's efforts to realize a potential that was longing for development. Now—one undergraduate and two master's degrees later—there is a counseling center at National Presbyterian Church that "speaks love." Other lay persons are following Mary Jane's example in obtaining advanced degrees and providing healing through sound professional counseling undergirded with Christ's therapeutic gospel.

I don't need to tell you how proud John is of Mary Jane. He laughs when he says, "Submission means learning to iron your own shirts," but he is very serious when he tells people about the ministry his wife is performing for Christ. John's giving of himself for his wife and Mary Jane's subjection to the nurturing love of her husband have done beautiful things in their marriage and in the body of Christ.

So I am to be in subjection to the love my husband gives

me: love that builds and nurtures and has its source in Christ. I give myself to him as he does to me. This is not domination; this is foot washing. This is following Christ in His servant role—not just woman to man, but person to person, heart to heart. This kind of mutual submission is beautiful and out of it comes a mutual reverence to Christ.

But I am not saying it is easy. In our many years of marriage, my husband and I have had to learn to be submissive and adaptable with each other. It certainly didn't happen automatically the moment Louie's father pronounced us man and wife. Fortunately, we started out believing that even though we were madly in love, marriage was going to be work and part of the creative task would be an ongoing process of mutual adjustment to each other. Not an easy thing, since each of us is strong—and stubborn—in our own way.

In 1 Corinthians 7:3 we read: "Let the husband render unto the wife due benevolence: and likewise also the wife unto the husband" (KJV). We've been working on that, and it has demanded meekness—God's gentle strength—in both our hearts.

In order not to get lost in each other, we have had to speak up about our individual needs. I'm thinking of my need to communicate with my husband and to feel we are in step emotionally. Now that takes time, and we have very little of that. So Louie has had to adapt to my need by carving time for communication out of his busy ministry. We have had to schedule time together on a regular basis and then fight the pressures of life that intrude on that time. It has never been easy, but neither of us would have it any other way. Communication, a big part of the work of marriage, has paid off. It nurtures our relationship. Enormously.

And I have had to adapt to Louie's needs—especially to his drive for his calling, which I used to fear might gobble him up, and at the same time, to his need for quiet and escape from the relentless demands of his ministry. His natural fascination with things mechanical creates an almost insatiable need to design, build, and tinker; yet these are characteristics I have come to accept and respect as part of the Louie God created. They are part of the man I love.

The truth is, we each have had to adapt to some things that have stretched us, but we are coming to appreciate the stretching as part of the God-designed complementariness of our lives. Not that our adapting is over. Far from it; we will be adapting to each other as long as God allows us life together. For the need to adapt is inherent in life, and adaptability is an inherent quality of meekness, of God's gentle-power in our lives.

One area where Louie and I have been learning to adapt in tandem is with our now-grown children. Since our daughter has married and our three sons have gone off to college or graduate school, we are definitely in a new season. We are alone in the house for the first time in twenty-five years, and loving it! But that isn't all. There are moments when we must consciously let go and take our hands off what does not belong to us: our children's lives. These "let go" muscles are relatively new and tender and sometimes become sore as we exercise them rigorously in this new season. We often find ourselves reminding each other that letting go really doesn't diminish love; it enables love to be.

Like most mothers in this world, I've done my share of dreaming about the future of our four offspring. Yet even though I have kept my dreams to myself, I'm not sure it's good for parents to have specific dreams for their children. That's forcing a goal on them in words they may not hear but will nevertheless sense, and they should have goals of their own.

I can't help thinking of another mother who, like me, "treasured all these things in her heart" and no doubt had glorious dreams for her Son. Was meekness hard for her, too? Did she struggle when it was time for her to give up her dreams so that God's plans for her Son could be fulfilled? And did she finally realize—as I must—that being a parent means molding children into themselves, not into what we may need for ourselves? I think she did. And with God's help, I, too, am putting my dreams to rest. Only one remains: that they will be the people God means for them to be. There can be nothing more.

What can I do for my children? The answer is obvious, and I accept it. I must be like a mother bird sitting quietly, patiently, on the branch of a tree, watching as her young take to the air. No longer does she hover over the nest, offering the fluttery protection of her wings. That time is past. Now she preens her feathers with motherly pride as she watches them take flight. She sits quietly, confidently, on the branch, refusing to interfere with the process that makes them strong and free. If there is real danger and they call, she is ready to go to them in an instant. But she is also ready to sit and watch and trust.

Dear Jesus, I'm not as patient as the mother bird, but it helps me to think of her quiet strength, her respect for her

young, her meekness. That's what I need more of, Lord—
this meekness adaptability, this inner strength—this bend-
ing to Your will.

I can no longer ignore this Beatitude, Jesus. In fact, now
that I understand what meekness really is, I like it, and I'm
asking You to put more of it in my life. You know how much
I need it.

Happy is the woman who does not hide her gifts and
strengths, but allows God to develop and channel her
strengths for His own good purposes. This woman has
gentle-power. She is secure enough to give and receive, to
live in a mutual relationship of submission that truly honors
Christ. Like her Master, she is genuinely meek, not weak—
strong enough inside to be adaptable outside. Happy is
she, for the earth is given to those who do not grasp at life
for themselves, but who freely embrace life for Christ and
others.

5

Happy are those who are hungry and thirsty for true goodness, for they will be fully satisfied!

Matthew 5:6

Blessed are they which do hunger and thirst after righteousness: for they shall be filled.

Matthew 5:6 KJV

What We Seek, We Become

I have to dig deep into this Beatitude. At first it seems obvious. Don't we all want to be good? And don't we feel much better when we do the right thing?

But there's more to these words than I see on the surface. I've been influenced by my life and its conveniences here in the United States. If I'm thirsty, I drink; if I'm hungry, I eat. Frankly, I don't give these needs much thought, because they are satisfied so easily.

Suppose, though, that I lived in a desert land where water was scarce and one crop failure could mean starvation? Ah, yes, what about hunger and thirst under those conditions? Now I begin to see a difference. Hunger and thirst become driving, powerful, urgent needs. They motivate my life and everything I do. I no longer simply *want* food and drink—*I must have them!* Without them I can't survive. And underneath all our modern conveniences, this is still true.

It is true of the spirit, too, and that's really what Jesus is telling us in this Beatitude. He's saying that it's not enough simply to *seek* goodness. Spiritually we crave it. This world is our souls' desert, and unless our souls receive the quenching, nourishing qualities of goodness, they will perish.

But what is this righteousness of God our souls crave?

The commonly accepted form of righteousness in Jesus' day was pretty much centered in ritual. It was measured by outward standards. People were expected to keep certain rules, and for that reason, many did. Perhaps it is even fair to say that righteousness was like a fine piece of clothing someone would put on, but which wasn't really part of the person. It was a counterfeit piety and could never satisfy the inner hunger of the soul.

In such a ritualistic setting, Jesus turned the whole concept of righteousness upside down (or right side up!). He taught that true righteousness was rooted in a genuine love for God and man and that it involved our inner motivations and feelings. Jesus promised that true righteousness would fill a person's deepest needs—not with material goods; not with an easy way of life; not with something of limited value that can be taken away, but with the joy and contentment that comes from doing God's will. Righteousness is not an option for the life of a soul: It is a necessity, as breathing is to the body. Take away God's righteousness, and the soul of any person suffocates—and ultimately dies.

During the seventies we talked a lot about the generation gap, and although we may not be as verbal about it in the eighties, it nevertheless exists. One of the reasons for it is a difference in values.

So many of our young people are disillusioned by their parents' obsession with the things money can buy. They might very well agree with the unknown writer of 2 Kings 17:15 (KJV) when he said: ". . . they followed vanity, and became vain." And how true these words are! If we seek power and prestige we become obsessed with being in the "right" places with the "right" people. If it is only pleasure we seek, we become shallow and silly. If money is our goal, we become materialistic and hard. While some families seem to grow closer together over the years, others are torn apart by what they seek: Rebellious, disappointed children trying to pull down the expensive roof their parents have put over their heads; parents giving their children every-thing, except themselves.

I'm reminded of Pam, a lovely girl and the only child of parents who gave her every physical blessing they could buy. The only thing Pam didn't have was a warm, loving relationship at home, and she needed that above all else. But closeness takes time, and Pam's parents were too busy making money to give her their time. Closeness means a commitment, too, but that had already been given to a corporation. As friends of the family, we saw what was happening, but there was no way to communicate our concern. Where there is a difference in values, there is also a difference in language. So it was no surprise when our phone rang late one night and we learned that Pam had run away.

I wish I could tell you there is a happy ending to this story, but I can't. Pam's parents know where she is, but they are unable to reach her "where she lives." Fortunately for Pam, she's young, and we still pray she will find happiness in her life; but I don't think she'll go looking for it among "things."

It isn't only materialism that leads us astray. A very subtle form of secularism can slip right into the church. A friend wrote us:

Some time ago, a friend was introducing me to his congregation, which I was to address. He went on and on about the great work I was involved in throughout the world. Some of it was true, but some of it was untrue, and practically all of it was exaggerated.

It was embarrassing because my wife and six children were present. Later they said, "We didn't know he was talking about you, dad." My greatest concern, however, was that none of the credentials which qualified me to speak had anything to do with faith in God—it was all numbers. People I knew, influence, and where I had been. We are always seeking a reputation, while Christ made Himself of no reputation.

"Religious" people especially need to be in touch with their spiritual motivations. This is the only way they can be sure they are seeking God and not their own reputations.

Lord, I'm so glad You didn't say, "Happy are those who *are* good. . . ." Who can possibly claim that! Not I! But You said, "Happy are those who hunger and thirst after goodness." Quite a different thing!

There have been times when I have hungered and thirsted for more of You in my life, Jesus. As I look back over the years I can see that these have been the best moments. Unfortunately there have been other times when I've been caught up in silly things that had no real meaning, and they left me with an empty heart. So the practical truth of this Beatitude is becoming very clear to me. Our happiest moments are those spent in seeking You and following Your Way in life. Long ago someone remarked that we become like the things we want most in life, and I have found that to be true. If it's money we want, we'll find a way to get it; but it will also get us.

It happened to a girl I knew when we were teenagers. She knew exactly what she wanted out of life: money and security, and plenty of both. Because she had high moral standards, I knew she wouldn't compromise them to reach her goal. But she was also very determined, and I never doubted that she would get what she wanted. She made it to the top of her profession on her own and on her enormous talent. Then she married a wealthy man. She had everything she wanted, or so it seemed. Then strange things began to happen to her life. It was no longer her own. Her days were crowded with meetings, managers, contracts, and endless red tape. Boards were formed to handle her money.

This woman was a warm, caring person who loved her family, but she found less and less time for them. Her possessions were possessing her, and she was becoming just another one of them. When she finally realized how trapped she was, she began to fight for her freedom. With the honesty that was typical of her, she began to search her spirit, listening for some inner voice. And the voice was there: faint, because her spirit had gone unfed for a long time, but perceptible.

My friend made changes in her life. It took time, and it took courage. Most of all it took faith—faith in Christ's promise that she could be filled and satisfied instead of empty. She began by saying no to some of the things in her life. She realized she didn't have to spend all her time making money. She didn't have to worry about security. She even considered what might happen if she lost everything. *Everything?* Well, she found she could live without her possessions, but not without the people she loved. As long as she had God, her husband, and her children, she was rich. None of her possessions had any lasting value, and once she was willing to let go of them, they lost their hold on her.

Jesus kept His promise to my friend—He always does. As her appetites changed (and appetite is what this Beatitude is all about) her life began to have meaning. Her days were spent with the people she loved and she found joy in the things they did together. She's still a wealthy woman, but she had learned, as Christians should, to wear her possessions loosely. Her guide is 2 Corinthians 9:8 (TLB):

". . . there will not only be enough for your own needs, but plenty left over to give joyfully to others." To her, it means that a person's possessions can be used to bless others. This is what gives them value. My friend is sensitive to human need; she hungers and thirsts to ease it. And in the act of giving she is, at last, finding the satisfaction she has always sought. The emptiness is gone; her life is filled with the contentment of following God's will.

I remember another woman who sought fame. Somehow she felt that if she could make it big in her profession, she would have everything she could ever want. She was so lovely, so talented, so filled with potential as a human being, and she traded it all for a promise that never came true. She made it to the top, all right, and she had more fame than she could handle, but her spirit went hungry. At the peak of her career she was a lonely, disillusioned woman trying to find warmth in a cold, materialistic world. So she kept climbing higher, reaching out—but for what? She never seemed to know, and neither did any of us who loved her. We were aware of her loneliness, her spiritual and human need, and we tried in our fumbling ways to help, but she always seemed just beyond our reach. If only she had been able to put her inner needs first, but her life ended, much too soon. It may seem odd to say that she died from starvation of the soul, but I believe she did.

There are some things in life we cannot understand, and her tragedy is one of them for me. I simply have to give it to God. But whenever I remember my friend—and I often do—I pray that God will use me in the lives of the women I know. I'm not clever or witty or full of special wisdom, but one thing I know, both from my own experience and from those who are close to me: Happiness doesn't come from money or fame or achievement. It comes from God, and the more we seek Him and His ways—the more attention we give to the hunger of our soul—the more fulfilled we will be.

Fulfilled: Now that word has a familiar ring. Yes, it's a word we hear a lot today.

In the past ten or fifteen years many voices have been telling us how important it is for us, as women, to be fulfilled. The goal is agreed upon, but the methods urged to reach the goal differ greatly from voice to voice.

About ten years ago I read *Fascinating Womanhood* by Helen Andelin, which was a first of a kind for me. I remember that she advised women to find fulfillment by gaining "celestial love" from their men. In his book *The Apostle Paul and Women in the Church,* Don Williams has a chapter titled "A Survey of Contemporary Views." Concerning Helen Andelin's celestial-love theory, he writes: "[It] is accomplished through a clever insight into the male ego. The message is simple. Find out what a man wants and needs, give it to him, and he will worship you forever." By 1973 Helen Andelin's book was in its twenty-second printing. Although I didn't share her concept of fulfillment, I read her book, and obviously, so did many others.

In much the same vein, Marabel Morgan wrote her number-one best-seller, *The Total Woman.* Her philosophy states that while women need to be loved, men need to be admired, and Mrs. Morgan urges women to find fulfillment by adapting to this difference: "A Total Woman caters to her man's special quirks, whether it be in salads, sex, or sports."

And as the woman adapts, "He in turn will gratefully respond by trying to make it up to her and grant her desires."

I appreciated the author's emphasis on a woman's being responsible to God first. I also welcomed her call to communication and her theological base for sex: "The creator of sex intended for his creatures to enjoy it." To that I say, "Indeed." But I struggled all through the book—not so much with the "adapting" and "catering," but with the inner motivation for doing so. To me it meant doing some right things for the wrong reasons, a game of getting what you want rather than serving in love. I missed the concept of husband and wife ministering "to one another, out of reverence for Christ."

In *All We're Meant to Be* Letha Scanzoni and Nancy Hardesty give an in-depth biblical pitch for "transcendency" as their ideal for feminine fulfillment. They base their view on Galatians 3:28 (RSV): ". . . there is neither male nor female; for you are all one in Christ Jesus." By *transcendency* the authors mean that men and women stand on equal footing as fellow members of the Kingdom of God. Marriage is a covenant, and motherhood is a choice in response to the call of God. Letha Scanzoni and Nancy Hardesty believe that as a married woman is fulfilled in the body of society, she will be better able to love herself, her husband, her family, her neighbor.

Other voices speak strongly of submission or of "God's divinely appointed order": "Wives, rejoice in your husband's authority over you! Be subject to him in all things. It is your special privilege to move under the protection of his authority. It is within this pattern of divine order that the Lord will meet you and bless you. . . ." as the way toward fulfillment and blessing.

We also hear a voice from the secular world. Betty Friedan, through her book *The Feminine Mystique,* published almost twenty years ago, awakened many women to the concepts of identity and fulfillment. As a reporter Betty Friedan sensed a high level of frustration among women who felt locked into the traditional female role of wife and mother. Beneath the frustration, she found a void, a basic absence of identity. Our society blamed it on too much education, a loss of femininity, and sexual fulfillment. But to Betty Friedan, the culprit was the widespread acceptance of "The Feminine Mystique," which held that women were inferior to men. This "mystique" gained support from Sigmund Freud when his definition of woman gave the traditional view a new scientific base. Woman, according to this definition, would fulfill herself—and find compensation for her biological inferiority—by being a wife and mother. She would live her life through her husband and children.

Betty Friedan disagreed. She believed that a woman needs her own identity. "The only way for a woman, as for a man, to find herself, to know herself as a person, is by creative work of her own," she wrote. But she has begun to take a second look at her views, as shown in her book *The Second Stage.*

So we hear voices telling us that fulfillment comes through submitting, through adapting and catering, through finding creative work of our own. But there is more, and here I'd like to quote Don Williams, author of *The Apostle Paul and Women in the Church:* "What we learn then from these texts [Paul's teaching throughout the New

Testament] is that the Gospel triumphs. It is the last word. The unity and equality of the sexes stand on salvation by grace alone which makes us brothers and sisters in God's family . . . we are to live equally before God and with each other while recognizing our differences. In this respect the diversity of the sexes is sustained. Unity and equality in diversity . . . is the result."

In other words, we find our destiny, our fulfillment as men and women, when Christ claims us and frees us to become the unique persons He created us to be. Remember—it was to disciples, both male and female, that Christ said, "Blessed are you when you hunger and thirst after God and his righteousness. You will be satisfied."

It is so simple: Men and women are fulfilled as they seek God and His goodness, when they feed their souls' hunger with the opportunity to love one another. For some women the way of loving service will be marriage and a family, which is a creative career in itself. For others it will be a career outside the home. For still others it will be both— which it has been for me, but not simultaneously. God has a place and a task for us, no matter what our season of life. Years ago I knew a season for birthing and raising our four children, and it was enormously creative and fulfilling. Now the children are gone, and while my first human priority is the work and joy of my marriage, I have time for other tasks as well.

My husband encourages me in my new part-time involvement with the House Subcommittee on Human Rights. He encourages me in my writing, and any other venture that is part of my seeking after God and His will for my life. This is part of my spiritual identity; this is my hunger and thirst.

Of course, each season has required its share of toil and sacrifice, but I am absolutely convinced that sacrifice is always a part of one's fulfillment.

Psalms 34:8 (KJV) tells us to ". . .taste and see that the Lord is good. . . ." As we cultivate a taste for Him and His right ways, our appetites will change. Spiritually it means giving up junk food and eating simple, basic meals that leave us satisfied, filled, and ready for life. And once we have tasted the kind of satisfaction that comes from following Him we'll want more—and more—and more.

Lord, give us ravenous appetites for You and Your right ways. Help us not to spend the brief days of our lives seeking silly things that can never honor You and that leave us shallow, empty people. As we go from season to season, give us courage to follow wherever You lead, trusting You for our fulfillment and for our very lives. What we seek, we become. Thank You for the glorious promise that as we seek You—crave You—we will become more like You. And that will be real fulfillment and joy!

6

Happy are the merciful, for they will have mercy shown to them!

Matthew 5:7

Blessed are the merciful: for they shall obtain mercy.

Matthew 5:7 KJV

Lord, Make Me Generous

The simple, direct words of our Lord have a way of digging into my complacent life and stirring things around. Like leaven in a loaf, they make me stretch and grow. It's not an altogether comfortable experience—change rarely is. Shall I come back to the Beatitudes another time? No. Without change, there can be no growth. So it must be.

Right away I run into trouble, because I'm not sure what mercy is. Or how it works. Or what it will do to my life. *Mercy* can mean "kindness," "compassion," "forbearance." But the word is rarely used anymore, and my mind

keeps tripping over it. It's too dramatic, too big, for everyday life and seems to belong to a crisis: ". . . God, have
mercy on a sinner like me" (Luke 18:13). It belongs there.
Mercy is a God-sized word.

Perhaps another word, another translation, will help.
Yes, here it is: *generous.* That's a person-sized word. Happy
are those who are generous with others—God will be generous with them.

All right, then, what about generosity? As I turn the word
over in my mind I immediately think of giving—giving
things, money, time. "Happy birthday, dear." "It's just
what I wanted!" "Sure, I'll help out." "We gave at the
office."

Yet something tells me that Jesus was talking about a
deeper, more demanding kind of generosity. What else can
I give? my hands, my mind, my attention, my love, my
understanding? Even more? Happy are those who give lavishly of themselves. Yes, I think that's what Jesus meant.

Suddenly my thoughts race back through the years. My
husband and I were very young, and everything was new.
Life seemed to come rushing at us all at once, and we met
it eagerly, head-on. Louie was in his first church, and the
congregation was new, too. The sanctuary wasn't built yet,
so having nowhere else to go, we held our meetings in our
home—two of the weeklies were men's prayer breakfasts at
7:00 A.M.! People were constantly stopping by with ideas,
concerns, problems. Then there was the phone, always the
phone. It would be understating the situation to say that my
plate was full, and so was my house! As a minister's wife
there was much for me to do, and I also was the mother of
four children, all of them under the age of five. I loved my

life, but it was wearing me out. I was hungry for rest and quiet, and there was none in sight.

Worst of all, I was starved for my husband. Longingly I recalled our student days in Edinburgh, when we used to walk for miles—talking, moving fast to brace ourselves against the chill wind blowing in from the North Sea. We had been so close then, but now I practically had to wave to him from across the room. I was proud of Louie and the work he was doing. I felt I was an important part of it. I was glad to share him with our family, our congregation—with the whole world, if necessary. But I wanted him, too!

It's never wise to hold your feelings in. They have a way of bursting into the open when you least expect it. That's what happened to me. I should have told my husband then how I felt, but I didn't want to burden him with my problems when he already was carrying so many others that seemed more important. So I kept quiet, until one night when we were getting dressed for the evening service.

Louie had come home very excited about a new project. Ordinarily I loved listening to his plans and his dreams, but that night my own frustration began to well up inside me. As he went on enthusiastically I could hear our front door opening and closing as the early birds began to arrive. I knew I had to speak, to tell Louis how lonely I was for him. *Right now?* something inside me said, disapproving. *Yes, now!* I thought. But instead of words, the tears began to fall. Again I tried to speak, and although I don't remember much of what I said, my husband apparently got the message. I was lonesome for him!

It was Louie's response that made me remember that night, years later, for he was truly generous. He waited until my tears stopped, and he listened to me, which wasn't easy to do with one hundred people sitting in our front room, waiting for the service to begin. Then he was generous in his attitude as he shared my need, confiding that he needed me, too. He was generous in his action as he promised, with God's help, to give me my time—no, to make sure we had our time together. And through the years, he has been generous in his determination to keep that promise. In spite of his hectic schedule, and often against enormous odds, he has kept our special times and our short trips away together as something sacred that must not be violated.

Many times I have heard Louie turn down invitations to meetings, speaking engagements, and almost anything that happens to fall on our night. "No, I'm sorry," he'll say, "but I have an important appointment for that night, and I want to keep it." And with those words he affirms me more than all the flowers and heart-shaped boxes of candy in the world could do. He knows I don't want things—I want him.

You really don't have to go far to get away. There are hundreds of glamorous places in the world and hundreds of exciting ads telling you how to get there and how much fun you'll have. Travel is a treat, and I love it, but it's expensive. Sometimes a husband and wife simply need to be and to be together. How often we forget about that because we put other, more material goals first in our lives. It's normal, I suppose, for a wife to want to help her husband get ahead, to make his dreams come true, but what good is worldly success if a husband and wife are strangers by the time they achieve it? Maybe a wife can do more than support a husband's ambitions. Maybe she can remind him that their life needs its quiet moments away from the pressures of work—and even the pressure of the family. Stillness, when it is shared with someone you love, can be a very rich experience.

I'm grateful for the many moments of stillness Louie and I have known together. Believe me, it wasn't always easy to arrange them, and there were times when we thought it would be simpler to forget the whole idea. But we didn't, and I hope we never will.

Sometimes we were so broke that after we paid a baby-sitter to come in for the evening, we didn't have a cent to spend on ourselves. But we didn't mind. We went for long walks in the lovely hills where our first church was being built. Then, for ten years, we walked the beaches of La Jolla. And now we stroll the city streets of Washington. We still take walks sometimes, between midnight and dawn, when there seems to be no other time to call our own. That's when we talk, eagerly pouring out all the feelings that have waited to be expressed. Sometimes we don't say a word—and that's all right, too.

Going away on short trips together has taken ingenuity, especially when the children were small. With a little luck, we could "child swap." That meant we would take care of our neighbors' children while their parents went off together for a weekend, and then a few weeks later our neighbors would return the favor.

Our need for baby-sitters has long passed, but we still have the need to get off by ourselves. For the first time in twenty-five years we are the only full-time residents at our house—and we love it. But as long as we are home there is the telephone, the doorbell, the distractions, and lots of part-time residents; so the difficulty of being together, apart and without interruption, is still quite real.

These times apart have helped to make our marriage a daily happening instead of a situation that exists. They give us time to be generous; they enable us to grow—individually and in our relationship to each other. (Thank you, Louie, for hearing me out that night. . . .)

I wonder, though: *Have I always responded to my husband's needs as generously as he has to mine?* I'm thinking of the times when he comes home unexpectedly for a half hour between counseling appointments, after a funeral, before a wedding. Sometimes I sense that he wants me to stop whatever I'm doing and sit down and listen to him or perhaps just be with him. Whenever I do, I'm glad. But sometimes I don't. Sometimes I'm too busy doing something to take time out to be someone to my husband. Those are the times I am not generous with myself. Generous with my services, yes, but not with me, and at that moment my husband couldn't care less about my talents as a homemaker or as a writer. He needs me as a friend, as a woman, as a lover—yet he has to play second fiddle to a vacuum cleaner or a writing pad.

Like most women, I like a clean house, but sometimes there can be too much housework and not enough home. We've all heard wives of late-working husbands say, "I don't want his money—I want him." Yet I wonder how many husbands would like to say, "Forget the house—I want a wife."

I admit I have a problem with neatness. I think it comes from being an only child and being brought up by my mother and grandfather. Affluent we were not, but we were very clean and neat, which is not so difficult with only three in the family. I grew up with a built-in sense of order, a pleasant way to live when you're all by yourself. But when you're part of a busy family and your husband is a gifted do-it-yourselfer whose work doesn't allow him time to finish his projects on schedule, an overdeveloped sense of order can be a drag.

My family is generous with my passion for neatness, yet I know it annoys them. In recent years I've learned to be more casual, but sometimes Louie has to take me by the hand and lead me away from a cluttered kitchen or an unfolded pile of laundry. "That can wait," he'll say. "This is our chance to do something together." He's right, and he's a good teacher.

Frankly, it bothers me to leave the dishes in the sink, and I don't like to see my husband run out of clean socks. But when he says, "Let's go," I ask myself, "What's the worst thing that can possibly happen if I don't clean the kitchen?" Leaving my work undone has never lost me a friend or caused the sky to fall in or the world to come apart. It has enabled me to give myself to the people and involvements I love.

Now, sometimes, it is I who have to make time for Louie. I have new responsibilities. I have board meetings, publishing deadlines, committee work, and I am learning what my husband learned long ago. I must say no to those things that would interfere with our special times together. It is interesting the way roles can change as the years go by. It's a good thing God's Spirit keeps us growing and flexible. This is all part of being generous and mutually submitted to each other.

Now I'm beginning to understand why Jesus urged us to be lavish in our giving. It's because generosity is a magical quality that seems to increase as it is used. I'm convinced that nervous breakdowns don't come from overwork (or overgiving), but from worrying about our work or keeping track of all our giving.

I find that the more I am able to give myself to Louie, the more I have to give. I do not wear out. I am not used up. Neither am I diminished as a person. I don't feel as if I am an appendage of my husband or my children. In giving myself, I discover who I am—and there is more to me than I thought. And the more I develop into a whole person—distinct and separate, yet one with my husband in spirit—there is more of me to give away. We can belong without possessing.

Again it is a matter of words and what they mean to us. If I think of a need as a demand, I'm going to resent it and pull away. But if I think of a need as an invitation to share the love and life of someone dear to me, I can only be grateful it came my way.

When a woman is married, she has a special and very beautiful opportunity to make generosity meaningful in a physical sense. I'm not talking about the sharing of tasks in a home, important as they are. I'm thinking about a man and woman who are very much in love, whose lives are joined in the sight of God, and who freely give their bodies to each other in a joyous ministry.

In sexual intimacy between a husband and wife, "For the wife does not rule over her own body, but the husband does; likewise the husband does not rule over his own body, but the wife does" (1 Corinthians 7:4 RSV). What a beautiful description of equality and mutual submission in the most intimate area of human encounter.

These days we hear so much about sex before marriage and outside marriage; one might wonder if sex is exciting only when it's illicit. The momentary tingle, the tang of guilt, the sudden splurge of passion—this is what we hear about sex. But sex is so much more and so much better.

Sex doesn't make the marriage, but it can certainly break it. Some marriages—too many marriages—suffer from an incomplete sex life. But that isn't the way married sex has to be; that's not at all what it can be. There are other kinds of marriages: marriages that constantly grow in honesty, friendship, goal-sharing, love, and the physical expression of that love. These marriages have soul!

Sex not only gives life; it celebrates the life God gave each of us. It becomes destructive only when it is cut off from its natural environment, commitment, and love. Then sex becomes unprincipled, fickle, selfish, hateful, even violent, almost as if it wants to destroy the life it was meant to serve. This unfortunately is the kind of sex we read about.

Only in marriage—a lifelong commitment where love is —can sex develop into the delightfully positive force God meant it to be. Here is where the excitement of sex really is. When a man and a woman make a lifelong covenant to love and cherish each other, they are affording themselves the time they will need to dismantle the barriers of restraint, shyness, defensiveness, and selfishness that exist between all human beings. It cannot be done in a night or with a rush of passion. It takes time to know and be known.

In a marriage, a man and a woman can discover the thrill

of trusting each other so fully that their freedom of expression reaches undreamed-of heights. Their intimacy becomes a sanctuary, a place where the soul of their relationship can grow through their physical oneness. No matter how many others they may share life with in the circle of family and responsibilities, they have this small, private world where they can offer each other their trust, their vulnerability, and the unrestrained affirmation of their love. But this kind of mutual ministry doesn't simply happen. It takes time, and it does not occur when it is limited to one brief encounter after another.

Generosity in the physical relationship of marriage brings each partner great dividends. In giving of themselves each receives in kind, and this reciprocity of love is beautiful beyond words.

Yes, generosity enlarges my life. It brings me closer to the people I love. But there is a world outside my front door, and I live there, too.

I wonder what would happen between nations, between races, between ordinary human beings if a Christ-like generosity influenced all our relationships. It wouldn't be easy, because when Jesus gives, He gives totally, with no strings attached. Could we Americans, for example, give aid to an emerging nation and resist the desire to tell those people how to live their lives? Could we put their interests ahead of our own if we had to make such a decision? Could we put our concern for basic human rights for all people ahead of our political expediency? If we could, and if people all over the world became convinced that we wanted everyone to reach his full potential as a human being, how different the human and international scenes might be.

Right here in our own country we could be so much more generous with each other. We mean well, but sometimes we don't give well—or enough. And now, in the eighties, we face an even greater challenge. With increasing government cutbacks in social services, we in the private sector have the responsibility—no! the opportunity—to do what Jesus has been telling us to do all along: minister to the poor among us.

I can imagine someone saying, "Now, wait a minute— that's a hopeless job. Besides, Jesus said the poor would always be with us, didn't He?"

Indeed He did. But He did not command us to wipe out poverty: He told us to minister to the "least of these" our brothers and sisters in Christ. There are so many real needs in our world, and although we can't answer them all, we must not use that as an excuse to do nothing. Christ urges us to find new creative ways to care for all people in His name.

Several years ago, Mother Teresa of Calcutta came to Washington to share her deep faith and tell us about her work among the dying and homeless of India. Louie and I were privileged to be among the guests at a small luncheon in her honor in the office of a mutual friend in the Senate. I wish I could find words to describe the effect Mother Teresa had on my life that day. I can't. Neither can Louie, for after the luncheon and a meeting that night at National Presbyterian Church, where this remarkable woman spoke to people from all over the city, my husband turned to me —his arms outstretched and his eyes brimming—and said: "What do we do with a person like this?"

Everything about Mother Teresa was so simple: her muslin habit—fastened with a safety pin—her face, her gaze, and especially her words. Even now, her answers to questions asked of her that day ring in my heart as models of gospel clarity and truth. When our host, the senator, a caring and sensitive Christian, asked Mother Teresa how she dealt with the lack of success in her work because such a high percentage of those she sought to help died in her arms, her answer was: "Jesus hasn't called me to be successful. Only faithful."

Those words have had a powerful influence in my life. When I hear about the overwhelming needs in our world —when I see some of them right outside my front door— the small efforts I make through a hunger committee, through an adopt-a-block program, through a covenant with the poor, seem desperately insignificant.

But then I remind myself that while I can never eradicate such a need, I can be faithful to what God asks of me day by day. And I thank Him and His servant Teresa.

A *Living Bible* is open on my desk, and my eyes just fell on 2 Corinthians 9:8, 9: "God is able to make it up to you by giving you everything you need and more, so that there will not only be enough for your own needs, but plenty left over to give joyfully to others. . . . the godly man gives generously to the poor. . . ."

But what about my friends and neighbors whose needs are not physical? Surely this Beatitude speaks to the need for a generous spirit, and I have much to learn about this kind of giving.

Perhaps the most generous thing I can do is to let people

be whatever they are. In other words, I must not judge them. When my neighbor's political views turn out to be the opposite of mine, I must not resent her. Not that we can't differ openly and honestly, but I must not try to change her into the person I think she should be. If I am to be generous about our differences, I must respect her ideas, however I may disagree with them. Generosity does not resort to manipulation.

Neither must I judge people by outward appearances. How a person speaks or looks, what he or she wears or doesn't wear, has nothing to do with what kind of person lives on the inside. Many years ago, when we lived in California, Louie and I learned how important it is to take that second look. One evening we went to a dinner party where all the other guests were either students or young people employed by the university near us. In fact, we were the only over-thirty guests there, and we felt like outsiders.

The moment we entered the room, I felt my old habit take over. In one quick glance I sized up everyone, or so I thought. It was during the sixties, and believe me, there was a lot to glance at: long hair, bare feet, strange clothes. After a while I didn't even notice these things, but at first I felt uncomfortable. I didn't seem to fit in.

Well, as the evening progressed and the conversation relaxed into honesty, we all discovered that our differences were quite superficial. One by one the barriers of age, dress, and life-style broke down, and we took a second look at each other. We were very much alike. Underneath some rather unusual exteriors, our fellow guests were warm, sensitive, concerned human beings who were very generous about accepting the two misfits in their midst. My split-second glance on coming into the room had been all wrong. I realized that the biggest hang-up didn't belong to the boy with the longest hair or the girl with the shortest skirt. It belonged to me.

Friendships began that night as we shared our similar joys and concerns. We found we had our differences, too, but we were able to talk about them honestly. We were learning to give each other the right to be ourselves.

Now I can see that generosity means opening yourself up to others. But what about those others, the receivers? Suppose they aren't there? What do we do with our generosity? Giving is only part of Christ's Beatitude, and if someone refuses what we offer, it hurts. Perhaps, then, some of us need to work at being generous receivers.

I learned a lot about receiving from the women in the congregations we have served, for they have been such generous givers in my times of need. I have learned still more from a good friend, a woman my mother's age. For some lovely reason, God must have put me "in her basket," because she has done so many kind and truly helpful things for me that I've lost count. And that's the way she wants it.

At first it was hard for me to accept so much generosity. My independent streak got in the way, and I began to feel uncomfortably indebted to my friend. I wanted to return her gifts in tangible ways, and of course I couldn't. Being a sensitive person, she realized how I felt, and one day she had a talk with me.

"Colleen, I get a lot of pleasure out of doing things for you," she said. "If only I didn't have to worry about your feeling of indebtedness, think of the fun I could have!" I couldn't believe it: She made me feel I'd be doing her a favor by accepting her deeds of love!

I did some thinking and praying, and gradually my attitude began to change. I put myself in my friend's place and realized how I feel if someone accepts my generosity with a frown on her face. And if a friend returned my favor tit for tat, like some kind of duty, it would make my generosity look like a pompous gesture done for show. But my friend gave freely and lavishly of herself, responding to my needs as she saw them, and that made me realize that the best way for me to be generous was to become a good receiver.

There is so much God wants to give us—not only for our needs, but because there will be ". . . plenty left over to give joyfully to others. . . ." God wants to show us how to minister to the poor in obedience to Him; how to express our love for our family, our friends, our fellowman and the whole world. And as we open up to each other in love and in caring, we will be more open to Him. Then His Spirit can move among us, soothing our cares, ministering to our hurts, uniting us in love, increasing our awareness of each other. In short, God wants to teach us how to be happy, generous people—and that's too good an offer to turn down.

Happy is the woman who is generous with her love and understanding, her possessions, and her very self. Because she becomes a part of the lives of those she loves, and because her happiness comes from her sharing, she receives even more than she gives, and God will be generous and merciful with her.

7

Happy are the utterly sincere, for they will see God!
Matthew 5:8
Blessed are the pure in heart: for they shall see God.
Matthew 5:8 KJV

Take Away the Shadows in Me, Lord

Pure in heart . . . pure in heart. . . . What do these lovely, familiar words mean to me, a wife, a mother, a woman concerned about the world? Do they mean I am to be spotless, perfect? If so, I'll stop now—no need to go on.

But wait. Surely our Lord was describing something more attainable for me. The concept of purity tumbles around in my mind. Then I look into the New Testament, where I find that purity is mentioned twenty-seven times. Gradually I reject the idea that *purity* means "perfection." Instead, it seems to mean "genuineness, sincerity, honesty, a singleness of mind and purpose." Or in the more concise words of Søren Kierkegaard, "Purity of heart is to will one thing."

Perhaps *transparent* is another word that describes purity. Yes, I like that. To be pure in heart is to be a transparent person: a person with no shadows or double meanings, one who says what she means and means what she says. I like people who do that—people who don't hedge, who take a stand, even if turns out to be unpopular. I can think of many heroes and heroines who were transparent people.

But what about ordinary human beings meeting life's ordinary situations? What about someone like me?

One day last summer, Jamie, our youngest son, who is about to graduate from college (where did all those years go?), called me on being less than transparent in one of these "ordinary situations."

We had just moved from a rented house in the city to a nearby row house we had decided to buy. Our new house is a wonderful one-hundred-year-old place with "great bones," but in need of much love and care, which, loosely translated, means hard work.

Jamie had come home for vacation just in time to lend his 6'3" and 190 pounds of pure energy to the task, and he was a great help. Each morning, as we surveyed what had to be done, I'd choose a Jamie-sized job and say: "Shall we do this . . . ?" And then again the next day: "Let's tackle this, shall we?"

Finally one morning Jamie looked me squarely in the eye and, in a firm voice that I knew meant business, said: "Mom, when you say, 'Shall we . . . ?' you really mean

'Would you . . .?' So why don't you ask me straight out— okay?"

Thank you, Jamie. It was a little thing only slightly less than transparent, so subtle I didn't notice; but you did, and you were right.

If we are going to say what we truly feel about the big things in our lives, then we must be careful to be honest about smaller matters. That isn't easy to do today, because we live in a world that urges us to play it cool. "Don't wear your heart on your sleeve." "Don't leave yourself wide open." "Don't get involved." Sound familiar, don't they? That's the kind of advice we all get from people who mean well. We may even catch ourselves saying the same words.

Jesus wasn't cool, and I don't think He wants us to be. When He calls us to become pure in heart, He's telling us we have to take some risks. If we're going to express ourselves truly, honestly, that means we'll have to expose ourselves and be vulnerable. Someone may take advantage of us. We may be misunderstood. We may get hurt. Yet that's part of being transparent. Nobody said it was easy.

Jesus, I know You understand, because You lived through it. You weren't one of those "now I have to be frank with you" persons who use truth like a dangerous weapon. But You were honest, no matter what it cost You. Remember when You told Peter that he would deny You? And he had just promised he would never turn away from You. But You had to tell him the truth about himself, and later he understood why. You were telling Peter that he wasn't perfect, that he was even a coward at times—and that You still loved him.

Because You were honest, sometimes You had to hurt people: the scribes, the Pharisees, some of Your followers and Your close friends, even Your family. But Your honesty was always combined with love, and I think that's what made the difference. You hurt only to heal, and everyone could see that love was Your motivation. It must also be mine.

Now I understand what You are telling me in this Beatitude. It's not enough for me to get rid of the shadows in myself. And it's not enough for people to be able to see clear through me. They have to be able to see through me *to something else. I must let God's love be visible through my transparency.*

Wanting to express ourselves honestly doesn't make it happen. It's not that we're deceitful, at least not deliberately; but we're in the habit of speaking abstractly rather than personally. We've been taught that it's good manners to leave our feelings out of the things we say. So we try to ignore our feelings entirely.

What a mistake that is! You can't ignore your emotions. Turn your back on them, and they'll poke you in the ribs. Run away from them, and they'll trip you. Slam a door in their faces, and they'll break your windows.

Besides, what's wrong with feelings, anyway? God gave us the capacity to feel, so He must have had His reasons. Here in the Beatitudes He tells us how to appreciate feelings, understand them, and use them. He reminds us that feelings can become vital lines of communication between one person and another. If we become transparent, there will be no obstacles between us.

Because it is so difficult for us to give up the defenses we put between ourselves and others, we need help in tearing them down. We just can't do it alone. That's why the pilgrimage toward transparency isn't a walk for loners. I know, because I've been on the journey for the past few years, and I would have turned back many times had it not been for those who walked with me.

It's harder to lean than to be leaned on. It's harder to take the extended hand than to reach out with your own. It's easier to comfort than to allow ourselves to be comforted. We would rather dry someone else's tears than expose our own sorrows. Yet we can't really reach someone else until we ourselves have been reached.

Through the years, my whole family has helped me discover and remain in touch with my feelings. Now that the children are grown, whenever they come home we have our own encounter group right around our dinner table. It's something we started doing when they were little, and their openness has always challenged me to become more transparent.

I remember one evening, years ago, when I was in the kitchen packing the next day's lunches. One of our sons was keeping me company, and I had the feeling something was on his mind. He was talking casually about school, his friends, nothing in particular, until finally he got to the point: He was having a problem with one of his teachers. He couldn't put his finger on the cause of it, but he knew they were at cross-purposes, and it bothered him.

I listened, wanting to help him sort out what he felt, but not knowing how. My impulse was to soothe him, to minimize the problem: "Don't worry about it, son. It'll all work out." "Maybe you're exaggerating the situation." "Try not to think about it so much." But that wasn't what I really felt, and I caught myself before I allowed the moment to slip by.

When my son began to talk about his problem, it reminded me of something that had once happened to me. For a split second I had an urge to share it with him, but I hesitated because it wasn't exactly my finest hour I was going to describe. Perhaps it's only human for us to want to present only the best parts of ourselves to our children, so I almost hid my real self behind a lot of meaningless clichés. Then I realized that my son had had the courage to be honest with me. He had been totally transparent, and I wanted to respond to him in the same way.

So I told him about a conflict I had had with one of my high-school teachers. It had happened so long ago, yet as I described it I could still feel the pain of it.

I had a teacher who didn't like me. I probably had done something to irk her—although I didn't know what—or perhaps I reminded her of someone else. Whatever the reason, she made my life miserable with her belittling remarks. I actually dreaded going to her class every day, knowing that she'd humiliate me in front of my friends.

It would have been wonderful to tell my son that I finally got through to my teacher and we had a nice, long talk that cleared up all our misunderstandings. But that wasn't what happened. I had to suffer through that year in school and go on to the next.

I did learn something from the situation. Almost everyone in school accepted me as I accepted them—but there were a few exceptions, and there always will be. Life is like that. Now and then you'll run into someone who just doesn't like you, perhaps for reasons neither of you can understand, and there isn't anything you can do about it. Yes, it hurts, but that's all right. Life goes on, and we can learn and grow through our hurts.

I could see that my son was interested and also a little surprised. He had heard (too often, I'm afraid) of my past successes. But at that moment it was important for him to hear about one of my failures because it made him realize that I knew how he felt. There I was, standing at the sink while he was sitting across the room, yet in a way we were holding each other's hand. We were sensing each other's feelings even if we couldn't put them into words.

Self-censorship, holding back parts of ourselves, seems to be the greatest barrier between human beings. I think it even prevents us from getting to know ourselves. Too often we build up false images of what we are, until we become convinced the images are real. Then it's especially hard to face the truth, to see ourselves clearly, transparently. We're afraid we won't like what we see, and we think others will feel the same way. So we go along, handing out our counterfeit selves—and then we wonder why we can't touch each other anymore.

A few years ago some of the people in our church family felt they wanted to reach out toward each other, yet they couldn't. They decided they needed help. And so they began—very cautiously—to meet together in small groups.

I understand what the word *group* brings to mind. We think of people behaving peculiarly, even sensationally, perhaps letting down too many restraints along with their hair. We thought of those things, too. But we went a little further and learned that there are many kinds of groups, some more constructive than others. It depends on what people want to get out of them and what they are willing to give to them.

Our church groups have a distinct advantage. We know we are not qualified to do group therapy—we aren't interested in weird experiments; we aren't looking for company in our misery. We are Christians who want to experience more of Jesus Christ and to support one another in our quest. We are seeking Christ in ourselves and in each other. We are trying to become our genuine selves.

We have a friend named Gordy Hess. He is a clinical psychologist and a beautiful Christian who has worked with many groups, and we like the way he describes the group experience: "Christ calls us to be real, not religious." Gordy says, "Our purpose is to hold hands with each other as we walk through this difficult and sometimes lonely life. Because we belong to God, we belong to each other—we need each other."

In the beginning I had conflicting feelings about being in a group. While I longed for the close fellowship a small group offers, because in a large church there is such a need for more than the Sunday-morning hello, I also was timid about this new experience. But once I get my feet wet, I was there to stay. Since then I've been involved in many women's groups, and women from nineteen to seventy have been transformed from faces in the Sunday-morning crowd to my sisters in Christ. I share my life with them, and the love that flows among us is a very special gift from God. Louie and I also are part of a couples covenant group here in Washington, and I am hard pressed to find words to describe the support and commitment we receive from and give to this group. We are family.

There have been painful moments when I was forced to look at the flaws in myself that the others helped me to see, but even then I knew I was loved and accepted. And there have been moments of utter joy over the discovery of something worthwhile I could share with others.

It has taken time and patience, but in these circles of caring we all have learned to express our fears, our hang-ups, our delights. Gradually we are able to express the most important part of ourselves: our love for God and for one another. At last we are coming to the place where we can share each other's burdens (Galatians 6:2), which is what Christians are meant to do. Prayer has been a very real part of our experience, and believe me, after the searching moments we share with each other, our prayers are not just a lot of pretty words. They are real, and they come from deep within us.

Some beautiful things have happened in these groups as we became more honest with each other. Personalities have emerged and spiritual wounds have been healed as we allow Christ and His kind of honesty to work through us.

I remember Anne, a woman I came to know and love in a church we served before coming to Washington. The first time I spoke to her we were total strangers. She and her husband had serious problems, and having heard about some good things that were happening through some of the church groups, she called to inquire about them. She sounded desperate. We couldn't accomplish much on the telephone, so we arranged to meet a few days later.

Anne told me her story. She and her husband, Carl, had

been married about twenty years. They had four fine children and a home that appeared—from the outside, at least —to be happy and secure. Anne and Carl were close, and their love for each other was deep—no problem there. When it came to sharing their faith, that was something else.

It was startling for them to realize that they had such a problem at all, because both came from Christian homes. When they met, Anne was the daughter of a minister, and Carl was a young seminarian interning in her father's church. They fell in love and were married when Carl graduated from seminary. Anne, at eighteen, went from minister's daughter to minister's wife, a simple enough transition—or so she thought.

She kept telling herself that her life was trouble free. And why shouldn't it be? She knew all the answers: She had memorized enough Bible verses to fit anything life might bring her way; she could study the Scriptures in depth and find their prescriptions for her problems; and she knew every hymn in the book. Going through the motions of her role was a snap.

But inside Anne there was another person—a woman who could not squeeze life into a narrow mold. This inner person needed more than memorized Bible passages to sustain her faith. She needed to know the living Christ Himself and to feel His influence in her life. Not understanding how to reach out to Him, she waited for His touch. When it didn't come, she began to doubt that He existed.

The doubts increased secretly for many years until finally Anne couldn't stand being a skin-deep Christian any longer. One day she told her husband how she felt. Understandably Carl was hurt and confused. Never having known such doubts himself, he was unable to deal with Anne's. He seemed to think he could compensate for her loss of faith by spending more and more hours alone in his study praying, reading the Bible, and meditating. Feeling rejected and filled with guilt, Anne rebelled against religion altogether: no worship, no prayer, no mention of God.

Everything else in her life began to come apart after that. She and Carl disagreed on how to bring up their children. Carl, a gentle, loving parent, seemed to get closer to the children, whereas Anne, a strict disciplinarian, felt she was pushing them away.

The reason Anne decided to get in touch with one of our church groups was that she had a particularly serious argument with her husband. As she was trying to explain her beliefs, Carl interrupted her angrily. "For God's sake and the children's, find out what you *do* believe!" he said. He asked her if she realized what a bad example she was setting for their children. Filled with hatred for herself and convinced that she was a failure as a mother, Anne ran to her bedroom. Sobbing, not even realizing what she was doing, she began to cry out to God, asking Him to show her where to turn. That's when she remembered hearing about the church groups and the way they were helping some people.

Anne was such an unhappy woman when I met her. Just talking about her problems was a big step for her to take, and I admired her courage. It meant she had to come out from behind the facade that had sheltered and imprisoned her all her life. She was presenting herself—doubts and all —as honestly as she possibly could. It was not an easy thing to do. What made it even more difficult was that Anne saw herself as an ugly, unlovable person, when, in fact, she was truly lovely.

I reached out and touched her. "You're coming into your own as an individual, Anne. That's wonderful!"

She was surprised. I could see she expected some sort of reprimand.

"It's all right," I said. "God meant you to be an individual—it's about time you got to know yourself the way He does.

"God loves you very much, Anne," I told her. "And He loves you the way you are. So do I."

I suggested that she meet with a small circle of women who would give her the help and support she needed as she searched for her authentic self. I could see that the prospect was both promising and frightening. It was like a door held open to her, a door that led to—who knows? For a moment she struggled with her fears, and then she won out over them.

That night Anne told her husband she was considering joining a church covenant group. When she saw the tears come to his eyes she realized how much she had been hurting him over the years and how much he really loved her! Holding each other tightly, they felt the warmth and closeness that had been missing for a long time. Changes were already happening in Anne's life.

The women's group helped Anne in many ways. "They accepted me even when I told them about my doubts of God," she said. But she still found it hard to share her problems with Carl. His self-confidence and his spiritual tranquility made her ashamed of her own uneasiness. Gradually Anne began to realize that the best way to communicate with her husband was for both of them to join a couples' group where they could face their problems together.

It worked. As the communication lines between husband and wife began to open, they revealed that Anne wasn't the only one with problems. Carl had a few of his own, and as he became less defensive about them he began to sympathize with the anguish Anne had been experiencing. She was no longer alone.

During the past year Anne and Carl have faced situations and crises that would have wrecked them if they had remained so far apart. But now they are able to support each other through life's rougher moments. They not only feel their love for each other—they *live* it.

And God? Somehow, through receiving His love as it came to her through others, Anne has received God. She has had the encounter she desperately needed, and it has given her courage to be herself. She is not afraid to let others see the person God created. She is becoming a transparent human being.

"Sharing my faith and my life with friends who really care has been the most wonderful experience of my life," she told me recently. "I feel as if I'm floating on a cloud of friendship—a deep, warm friendship with Jesus and His people."

Now you can understand why I feel that Christ-centered groups can help us along our pilgrimage to transparency. Anne is one example, and there have been many others. Of course, group work is only one way, and it's not for everyone. A good friend of ours, who has come alive as a person and a believer during the past few years, says, "I don't need a group—my whole life has become a group experience."

And he's right: Just being with him is an exciting encounter with honesty. This should be the end result of every group experience.

As this chapter began, I quoted the words of Søren Kierkegaard: "To be pure in heart is to will one thing." The more I ponder the meaning of those words, the more convinced I become of the inherent health and wholeness of this Beatitude. For it's true that when any of us has conflicting loyalties, our energies are drained. We become confused and tense. I know this is so in my own life. If for any length of time I try to keep my eyes on two masters, my vision gets blurred. As my eyes flit back and forth between the two, neither image is clear. But when I slow down, prune away the conflicting loyalty, and look simply to God, the focus of both the vision and my life becomes sharp and clear again. And I am at peace.

Recently Louie and I were part of a seminar for ministers and their spouses. During the time set aside for discussion and sharing, one of the questions asked of us was: "What was your biggest failure in the ministry?" I really struggled for a few moments. For some reason the question bothered me. Not that we haven't had failures: We have had lots of them, and we feel no hesitation in talking about them, even laughing about them. But the way a Christian looks at success and failure is different from the way the world does. For the disciple, the only real success is in being faithful to the Master, not in keeping score, and that may not equate with worldly success.

Many years ago, early in Louie's ministry, we discovered that serving Christ and also trying to meet the demands of worldly success was like serving two masters. It blurred our vision, drained our energies, and upset our spiritual equilibrium. So somewhere along the line, we decided to put aside a concern for numbers, power, prestige. If such things came, we prayed they would honor God, but they would not be part of our goal. We have found, in these later years, that there is freedom and peace in "willing one thing." We have also found that seeking to be faithful to Christ takes everything we have.

Dear Father: Give us the honesty and transparency that makes us pure in our hearts. Simplify our lives until we are "willing one thing," no longer serving two masters, one inside and one outside. Help us to focus our vision on You until we truly become "the pure, who *see* God."

Amen.

8

Happy are those who make peace, for they will be known as sons of God!

Matthew 5:9

Blessed are the peacemakers: for they shall be called the children of God.

Matthew 5:9 KJV

Lord, Not a Holy Cover-up?

Peace—ah, yes, we see the word often these days: in symbols, on bumper stickers, on Christmas cards, and on buildings. One friend of ours uses it on his personal stationery, another has it written boldly across his front door. It's all around us, yet, what is it, this peace? And who are today's peacemakers? Whoever they are, Jesus says they are happy people, and they belong to Him. Happy are the peacemakers; they are the children of God.

Is peace something quiet, unruffled, perhaps unreachable? Are the peacemakers those calm, unshakable people

I often wish I could be like? And is there really a place for peace in this turbulent, pulsating world?

The word *peace* makes me think of summer vacations, of long hours when at last I don't have a schedule that has to be met, when the weather is warm and beautiful and I have time to hear the breeze moving in the trees. Yes, that's peaceful, but throw in a little rainstorm, let my work fill my days with busy moments, and exit peace! At least, that kind of peace.

But that's all right—because that's not the kind of peace Jesus is describing in this Beatitude. The peace we find in this world is dependent upon time, place, and circumstance. It comes and it goes. Jesus was talking about spiritual peace, the peace that comes from God. He spelled it out for us: "I leave behind with you—peace; I give you my own peace and my gift is nothing like the peace of this world" (John 14:27).

His "own peace" is described for us in two biblical terms. The word for *peace* in the Old Testament is *shalom,* which means a great deal more than an absence of war. It embraces all the characteristics of a life of peace: honesty, harmony, power or victory over destructive forces. It implies an honest peace that comes after an honest struggle. (I like that!) But most of all, *shalom* speaks of a beautiful relationship with God. It gives us both a vision for the future and a model for the life that is possible today.

The New Testament word for *peace* is the Greek word *eirene.* Again, it does not mean simply the absence of conflict. It is the peace Jesus spoke of when He said, "Peace be with you" and, "Go in peace." It describes a new relationship, something qualitatively different, between God and

His people, and between persons. And once we have this "different" peace, it never leaves us, no matter what happens in our lives or in the world around us. God's very own peace is an occupancy of the heart, a feeling that Someone is deep inside us all the time—a spiritual reaching out for God's hand and finding it there. That is peace.

Surely, then, if we are to become peacemakers, we must first of all be at peace with ourselves. In *The Violence Within* Paul Tournier says that each human being has a potential thrust for violence and a thrust for peace. At the very core of our beings, a war is being fought, and unless we daily yield these struggling parts of ourselves to God, we will eventually carry the battle out into the world. As Jesus said, ". . . if a household is divided against itself, it cannot last . . ." (Mark 3:25). Neither can we; our inner conflicts can bring the walls of our beings down around our ears.

That's what happened to some people I knew years ago. They were unhappy in their church because they objected to the minister's "politics in the pulpit." For instance, one Sunday the minister asked the congregation if they thought they could buy love *and* justice, and some members thought the love theme sounded a bit like some kind of communist propaganda. They thought a preacher should preach the gospel, but apparently without applying it to life.

Well, the unhappy members left the church and joined another one that was known for its strict emphasis on worship and its lack of social involvement. But still the people weren't happy. They had just as many complaints, although for different reasons. It was obvious that wherever these people might go, they would take their inner frustrations with them and become disturbers of the peace. Nor would they ever find peace anywhere until they found it within themselves.

When Jesus lives within us, His love brings the warring elements of our selves together into the whole persons we were meant to be. He frees us to be the "you" of you and the "me" of me. We can shake hands with our selves, and we have peace.

There's also something about inner peace that makes us want to spread it around. We want to bring it into our relationships with other people and eliminate the barriers between us. But that isn't always easy, and sometimes the process isn't what we usually think of as "peaceful." It may mean uncomfortable, even painful exchanges between us.

A few years ago Louie and I were visiting friends from another parish we had served. It was what we call a "warm-fuzzy" night—comfortable old friends combined with interesting new people to meet.

At Louie's table there were several new acquaintances, one of them a gifted artist whose work we both admired (but couldn't afford). Her name was Gail, and she was a lovely woman, full of grace as a person. From her husband, with whom I was sitting, I learned that she also had a busy homelife; when I asked about the size of their family, his answer was simply, "Boys—and numerous!"

Gail seemed to be a woman with everything. But of course we didn't know what was going on inside her, and at that moment she was in the midst of a terrible struggle between her home and her career. At first she had thought she could handle both and do a creditable job in each area. Then came the days when she couldn't cope, and the short straw always seemed to go to the boys and her husband.

Actually we all have days like that, even when we don't have a budding career to squeeze into our lives. But Gail was convinced that she was having more than a normal share of difficulty, and she was afraid it was hurting her family. On the night we met her, she was carrying a heavy burden of guilt in her heart.

I didn't know how Gail felt until a year later. Louie was one of the speakers at a regional ecumenical retreat, and Gail and her husband were there, representing their church. It was wonderful to see them again, and I was expecially delighted to learn that Gail and I were in the same small group that was to meet every morning for discussion and sharing.

At our group's first meeting we went from one to another, trying to put words around who we felt we were and what we thought was our main priority as a Christ-person. Everyone shared—except Gail. Throughout the meeting she blinked back tears. No one questioned her, but her silence let us know she was hurting. After the meeting, she stayed behind, and I could see that she wanted to talk. When we were alone, she told me what was bothering her, and would you believe it? *It was my husband!*

Apparently, at that "warm-fuzzy" dinner party almost a year ago, Louie had said something that cut Gail deeply. It seemed almost cruel. He had spoken of the need to balance a career and a family and of the danger that a profession might take up all of a person's life energy, leaving human relationships, and the family in particular, with the crumbs from the table. His remarks may have been general, but to Gail—at that sensitive moment in her life—they were crushing. Her mind began to play tricks with her: "Louie knew something"—he didn't. "My husband must have talked to him"—he hadn't. "Louie thinks women shouldn't have careers"—wrong again! Silently, all those months, Gail had kept her hurt inside herself, until now it had festered and grown out of proportion.

I understood what Gail had done, for I could remember doing the same thing: being hurt, usually through a misunderstanding, and instead of talking it out immediately, I embraced the hurt feelings—suffering inside for days, weeks, even months. Why do we do such things, when it's so much better to embrace a friend than a hurt?

Clearly, Gail had misunderstood Louie. I knew his feelings on the subject, and I realized that he hadn't been talking to Gail specifically, nor to women in general. He was speaking about all people: about businessmen who make money their god, about ministers who make success their thing, about himself and me, for we were having our own struggle to maintain a balance between work and family.

For months Gail had felt guilty and censured—unnecessarily. I tried to tell her that, but she wasn't about to be convinced, at least not by me.

It was a long day, waiting to see Louie alone. First there was lunch, and then the "discipline of silence" until dinner. (It really *was* a discipline for me that day!) Next came dinner, then evening vespers—and finally, cabin time! At last I could tell Louie about Gail.

When I told him, he was concerned—concerned that Gail had been hurting for so long, concerned that she was hurting still. Late as it was, he grabbed his flashlight and went looking for the cabin where Gail and her husband were staying. He was gone a long time, and I fell sound asleep.

The next morning, at breakfast, Gail's husband—a gentle giant of a man—rushed up to us and hugged Louie. "Louie, Louie," he said, "there is peace between my house and yours!"

Peace had been made the night before as Gail and Louie talked out their misunderstanding on the porch of Gail's cabin. At first it had been awkward and difficult for both of them. Now they were very tired and would need an extra cup of coffee. But the important thing was that they had been willing to suffer the discomfort that led to mutual understanding, to *shalom,* the peace that comes after the honest struggle. And then, as they talked, they really heard each other; they became peacemakers.

God wants us to mend these breaks in our relationships with others. Only when Jesus makes us whole can we begin to see that the world itself needs to be made whole.

Peacemakers are absorbent persons. When malicious words and gossip hit them, they go no further. Instead of gloating over the evil, they're like a great silencing chamber. Gossip hits them and is absorbed. Yes, they may feel the sting of it, but they don't need to pass it on. They smother it with love (1 Peter 4:8 [RSV]: ". . . love covers a multitude of sins").

I'll never forget seeing such a magnanimous spirit in action many, many years ago, while Louie and I were studying in Scotland. Billy Graham came to London to hold a crusade at the Harringay Arena. Since we had known Billy and the team back home, we were asked to come from Edinburgh to work with Dawson Trotman in follow-up—

which we did for eight wonderful weeks.

One night several of us squeezed into a small British car to accompany Billy to the arena. Billy was preaching that night, and I remember wishing he could have had a quieter ride, but we were excited and talkative. Then one of our group began to tell Billy about some unkind, cutting, terribly unfair comments a church leader had made about him in the newspapers. Apparently our fellow passenger felt it his duty to repeat them to Billy, but believe me, if I'd had a muzzle I'd have used it! I felt hurt for Billy, and I wondered how he could get up and preach after hearing such things.

For a long time Billy sat quietly. Then, thoughtfully and simply, as though he were speaking partly to us and partly to Someone Else, he said, "God bless that man. If I were in his place, I'd probably feel the same way about me."

As far as Louie and I can recall, that was all he said. It was more than twenty-five years ago, but we have never forgotten it. Many times, finding ourselves in similar situations, it has helped us to remember his words and his attitude. (Thank you, Billy!)

Jesus, that helps me understand what You meant when You said, ". . . Love your enemies, bless them that curse you . . ." (Matthew 5:44 KJV). I always wondered how I could throw my arms around someone who deliberately hurt me. Now I know it's not easy, yet it is possible—if I am a peacemaker. There is a difference between the action and the person, and I don't have to love them both.

Peace in our minds, peace in our close relationships, that's a good beginning. But if peace ends there—on the

inside—something is *very* wrong. Peace is a precious com-
modity, a part of our inheritance in Christ, but if we seek
it simply for our own comfort, it will lose its purpose.

We must remember that we aren't called to *keep* peace,
but to *make* peace. The inner peace Jesus gives us equips
us to go out into the world and bring its warring forces
together.

Increasingly, as a Christian, I am feeling that inherent to
peace in our own lives, and in our world, is a concern and
respect for human life because it is sacred. Peace is justice
for all—no matter what a person's class, sex, creed, or race.
When the poor feel they have no friends in powerful places,
it fosters frustration and violence. So peace means doing
what Jesus commanded: caring for the poor, the widowed,
the orphaned, the imprisoned. And through my small involvement in the House Subcommittee on Human Rights
as it holds hearings on religious persecution around the
world, I am growing in my conviction that a dedication to
peacemaking means raising our voices in behalf of the
voiceless ones of this earth and sharing the silent tears of
those who suffer. I am aware, too, that peace may also
require the risking of our lives for the sake of our brothers
and sisters. In short, I am learning that there is a cost to
being a peacemaker. When we walk the way of peace, we
should not be surprised to find a cross around the corner.

It's interesting to me that Jesus didn't say, "Blessed are
the peacekeepers." What a difference between keeping the
peace and making peace.

Keeping peace is passive: "Don't rock the boat." "Don't
get involved in controversy." "Sweep unpleasantness
under the rug." Peacekeepers often hide from problems,

crying, "Peace, peace!" when there is no peace and no one to make it. By ignoring conflicts, they actually make them worse.

"Making peace" is active, involved, aggressive. Peacemakers can see past personalities to the issues that must be resolved. They are open-minded and fair, eager to know what people are feeling and able to bring those with opposing views together. They are strong people who can take moral stands. They bring sanity out of chaos and confusion. They are bold, courageous. Sometimes they are persecuted for their courage, and on some rare occasions, they are honored. It was heartening to me that in 1980 the Nobel Peace Prize was given to Perez Esquivel, a committed Roman Catholic layman who dedicated himself to *Paz y Justicia,* the Latin American Committee for Peace and Justice. He is a man known for working in defense of human rights by nonviolent methods. He is a man of peace. I think of Anwar Sadat's courageous involvement in the Camp David peace accords, and I wonder if his death was part of the price for his desire for peace in the Middle East. I think of the mothers of northern Ireland—Catholic and Protestant women—raising their voices in behalf of peace in the midst of outrageous confusion and violence. And there are many more.

But whether we are praised or blamed because of our peace involvements is not the point. To be obedient to God, we must be involved in some way, for it is our Father's very nature to make peace. We call Him "the God of peace," His Son is "the Prince of Peace," and Paul says, "He is our peace." Peacemaking is what God does and what we must do as we follow Him.

Another part of peacemaking is evangelism. The Bible
tells us that God is out for the salvation of the world. As we
grow closer to God, we naturally identify with Him in His
desire to redeem His world. I think it was Clarence Jordan
who said, in his warm, picturesque way, "With all our
brothers and sisters in Christ we go into a family business
of redeeming the world for Him."

Certainly a sincere evangelist is a peacemaker. His or her
entire ministry is given over to reconciling people to God
through Christ. But we all can't be evangelists in that sense,
can we? Some of us—most of us—have no talent for speaking to masses of people. Some of us simply let God's peace
work in our lives and pray that it will fall like good seed in
the lives of those we touch each day. If we use every opportunity to share the gospel of Christ in a loving way that is
natural for us, we are the peacemakers—each one of us.

God uses each person's unique gifts and talents to reach
out to others. I'm thinking of a psychologist who was in-
strumental in helping a friend and her husband find peace
in their marriage.

Sue is someone I don't see very often. Actually, I don't
have to, because our friendship is always there when either
of us needs it. One day Sue called and said she needed it.
She was crying. I waited, not knowing what to say, but I
used those moments to pray for my friend and for Ed, her
husband. Their marriage had been in trouble for years.
They had serious financial problems, and both of them
were working to keep their two older children in college.
There was a crisis in the life of a younger child, and during
the past few years there had been a siege of illness and
surgery in the family. Life had been rough for Sue and Ed,

and instead of bringing husband and wife closer together —as rough times can do—it had driven them apart.

When Sue got control of her tears and was able to talk, she told me that their situation had come to a head the previous day. She and Ed had a terrible argument. In desperation they went to a mutual friends of theirs and ours —a minister who is now a clinical psychologist. This man is truly gifted by God in the art of counseling and generously filled with the love of the Holy Spirit. He was just what Sue and Ed needed.

First he asked Sue and Ed to be specific about all the things they resented in each other. Painful and humiliating as it must have been, they did it; and there it was—all the years of ugliness and hurt out in the open.

Then the counselor asked them to be equally specific in describing all the good things they saw in each other: the things that had drawn them together in the beginning, had made their marriage last for twenty years, and were still there. And as they probed among the ruins of their life, they began to see that there was still a lot to love in each other. As Sue put it, "We really have so much going for us."

I realized then that Sue's tears came from joy, from the relief of knowing that she and Ed could become whole again, in time. Our friend, the psychologist, had been the peacemaker in this couple's fragmented relationship.

Sue and I prayed for God's final touch of healing, for she and Ed had done many things to hurt each other in the way that only a husband and wife can hurt, and there was a deep need for forgiveness on each side. But they would have help. Jesus is the expert Forgiver and Forgetter, and He had come to live in them.

As I hung up the phone that day, I was grateful for all peacemakers everywhere. And I prayed that when I had the opportunity to serve, I would be ready. But I need to remind myself that while God calls us to be peacemakers, He does not guarantee success. One of the most poignant stories in the Bible is the account in 1 Samuel of Jonathan's efforts to bring peace to the relationship between two men he loved; his father, Saul, and his friend, David. The fact that he was not successful does not detract from the beauty of the story. Peacemakers may not always win, but they must always try.

Am I ready now? There really isn't any way to be *ready* to bring people together. Jesus is always ready. We simply have to let Him use us.

But some conflicts are so big. Where do we begin to reconcile them? I'm thinking about war—after all, you can't really think about peace without thinking about war. What can I do about it? What can ordinary people do to end war?

I read an unsettling statement in *Choose Life: A Statement on Disarmament,* a document: from the 1979 General Assembly Presbyterian Church:

> Finally, our sisters and brothers, we call to your attention the authoritative predictions that nuclear war by the 1990's is an increasing probability. . . . Even now, only twenty years separate us from the moment when we will be called upon to mark prayerfully the bimillenary anniversary of the coming to the world of our Lord and Savior, Jesus Christ, the Prince of Peace. . . . In what state shall we present

our planet to the Creator: shall it be a blooming garden or a lifeless, burnt out, devastated land?

That is a haunting question for me. I hate war—most people do—especially those who have lived through a war, lost a family member to war, or have seen their land devastated by war. The fact that I have three sons may have something to do with the intensity of my feelings. Yet I felt the same way before I had sons. I also hate tyranny and manipulation of persons, and there lies the moral conflict with which we struggle.

Still, there are things we can do as peacemakers. The Presbyterian Church Confession of 1967 puts it this way:

> The members of the church are emissaries of peace and seek the good of people in cooperating with powers and authorities in politics, culture and economics. But they have to fight against pretentions and injustices when these same powers endanger human welfare. Their strength is in their confidence that God's purpose rather than people's schemes will finally prevail.

We can pray for the leaders of our nation and for those of other nations. We can pray for the men and women who have the enormous responsibility of making decisions that affect the lives of so many others. May they be sensitive to the forces that lead to peace; may they be strong enough to suffer the discomfort of reconciling differences; and may they respect honest differences and not make conformity their only aim. May they, too, pray for guidance.

War does more than kill. It commits atrocities on the hearts and minds of the people who stay behind while their sons go off to fight. During times of war, propaganda convinces us that we are fighting subhuman people. A Japanese-American friend of ours went through a cruel ordeal during World War II. One day he was a respected friend and neighbor, and the next day he was whisked off to an internment camp as a so-called national-security risk. Many German-Americans suffered similar experiences. After the war, the Russians became the bad guys, and then the Chinese. Now it's the Russians again. That's what happens when we allow ourselves to become part of war's hate syndrome. It seems that only in times of relative peace are we able to see all the people of the world as our brothers and sisters.

We can support our country without hating those who disagree with its policies, because, for peacemakers, there is no enemy. We can aim to be like Jesus, hating the forces that cause war, but never hating our fellow human beings who are caught up in it.

But wars don't have to start. We don't have to hate or destroy. There is another Way. . . .

In the closing scene of the film version of the novel *Ben Hur,* the young Palestinian Judah Ben Hur is reached by Jesus the Christ. And Judah, a man whose life has been filled with hate, bitterness, and revenge, says simply, "He has taken the sword out of my hand." That's exactly what Jesus does when He comes into our lives. He takes the swords out of our hands. We no longer want to hurt. We want to heal. With His love in our hearts, we shall be able to make peace, and as God's children, we shall be unable to make war. That's the other Way. At least, in my own personal struggle of conscience, it is for me.

Jesus Christ is our peace.

Happy is the woman who truly longs for peace—within herself, within her family, and throughout the world. For she knows that strife begins within the human soul where parts of ourselves are at war against each other. Beginning with herself, she asks God to help her end the conflicts that lead to destruction. From there she seeks to reconcile the differences that exist among all human beings, even in the midst of love—perhaps even in her own family. Deeply happy is that woman when she sees that God is her peace and that through her words and witness she can be used by Him as a peacemaker.

9

Happy are those who have suffered persecution for the cause of goodness, for the kingdom of heaven is theirs! And what happiness will be yours when people blame you and ill-treat you and say all kinds of slanderous things against you for my sake! Be glad then, yes, be tremendously glad—for your reward in Heaven is magnificent. They persecuted the prophets before your time in exactly the same way.

Matthew 5:10–12

Blessed are they which are persecuted for righteousness' sake: for theirs is the kingdom of heaven. Blessed are ye, when men shall revile you, and persecute you, and shall say all manner of evil against you falsely, for my sake. Rejoice, and be exceeding glad: for great is your reward in heaven: for so persecuted they the prophets which were before you.

Matthew 5:10–12 KJV

Use My Brokenness

As I read this Beatitude again, I am stopped short. On the surface it almost *seems* that Jesus is saying, "Go out and seek persecution—you aren't a bona fide Christian until you do." But of course that *isn't* what He is saying. To court suffering is not healthy.

I think Jesus is being realistic. He knew the gospel He preached was so different from the way most people thought and lived that it would indeed invite misunderstanding and persecution. He is saying, in effect, "Be faithful—and be ready to pay the cost. Be glad you are on God's side. You're in splendid company. But prophets always have suffered and always will suffer for their faith."

Many people think persecution came only to the early Christians, but my interest and involvement in human rights and religious persecution has taught me that there are many places in the world where it's still dangerous to believe. When I look at a chart listing the ten most oppressive countries in our world, it reminds me to pray for my brothers and sisters who are at this very moment suffering for their faith. Many are imprisoned, their voices stilled. I am trying to understand what it means to "remember those who are in prison, as though in prison with them; . . . since you also are in the body" (Hebrews 13:3 RSV). I am learning to raise my voice in their behalf.

My chart also lists the ten countries in which one can enjoy the most freedom, and I thank God ours is among them. But I need to be mindful of tendencies toward religious prejudice in our own country. I must stand against them as well.

Persecution still exists here, and many of us later Christians will be asked to suffer for our faith. The acts of torment are more subtle than those the Romans used, but they can be very painful.

There is the social stigma that marks us when we refuse to join organizations that exclude certain people, the looks of guests at a dinner party when we don't laugh at their dehumanizing jokes, the ridicule a young person experiences when he refuses to go along with the group in unhealthy experiments. Love itself disturbs some people.

Chip, chip, chip—that's the way it goes these days. Hundreds of little jabs that chip away at our spiritual complacency, reminding us that we are not our own. We belong to Jesus, and there is a price we must pay.

> If we're humble, the proud and arrogant will call us foolish.
> If we're tamed by God, the self-made will call us weak.
> If we're transparently honest, we will irritate those who feel uncomfortable with the truth.
> If we're generous and those around us seek revenge, we'll be known as a soft touch.
> If we believe that God's ways are the best ways for mankind, we'll be called prudes.
> If we're peacemakers when others want war, we'll be called weaklings, even traitors.

Just as Jesus was persecuted, His followers will meet with opposition along the Way. Unavoidably the Christian life will be a rebuke to some, and people don't take kindly to being rebuked.

Christians were made to give and receive love, not to hate or lie in wait for an enemy. That's why, of all things in life, persecution is the hardest for us to bear.

But why does anyone have to suffer? Is it God's way of reprimanding us when we do something wrong? And if we do all the right things, will we automatically be exempt from this pain?

Intellectually we all know that the answer to those questions is *no*. Yet we often behave as if it were *yes*. Let suffering come into our lives, and we begin saying, "What have I done wrong?" Or worse than that: "Why is God punishing me?"

Suffering is a stubborn fact of human life. It comes to everyone, without discrimination. Disease, death, disasters, defeats—no person or family is immune. But not all suffering has value: What we suffer for can make a difference. Jesus didn't say, Happy are you when you suffer—period. He said, Happy are you when you suffer for the right causes. The crosses we make for ourselves by giving in to pressure and stress, or by worrying anxiously over the future, are not the crosses that come from God.

If I were to tally the score, I'm sure I'd find that most of my suffering has come from doing something wrong and not from doing something right for God. I make more mistakes than I like to admit. I've been thoughtless; I've hurt people; I've been selfish; and when I realize what I've done, I suffer. There is no joy in this kind of pain.

But even when I make careless mistakes I can feel God at work in me, showing me my weaknesses, pushing me to admit I was wrong, stretching me, and then finally giving me the grace to forgive myself. So there is some good in this kind of suffering, after all, yet it's not the kind Jesus is describing in this final Beatitude. He is speaking about the kind of suffering we will know only when we stand with Him and walk His Way. It is the outcome of *living* the Beatitudes.

One of our friends says, "Suffering takes away shallowness," and it is true that suffering seems to peel away the surface veneer of our lives to reveal the real person beneath. I love the conversation between the Skin Horse and the Velveteen Rabbit in the story *Velveteen Rabbit* by Margery Williams:

> "What is Real," asked the Rabbit one day when they were lying side by side near the nursery fender, before Nana came to tidy the room. "Does it mean having things that buzz inside you and a stick-out handle?"
>
> "Real isn't how you are made," said the Skin Horse. "It's a thing that happens to you. When a child loves you for a long, long time, not just to play with, but REALLY loves you, then you become Real."
>
> "Does it hurt?" asked the Rabbit.
>
> "Sometimes," said the Skin Horse, for he was always truthful. "When you are Real, you don't mind being hurt."
>
> "Does it happen all at once, like being wound up," he asked, "or bit by bit?"
>
> "It doesn't happen all at once," said the Skin Horse. "You become! It takes a long time. That's why it doesn't often happen to people who break easily, or have sharp edges, or who have to be carefully kept. Generally by the time you are Real, most of your hair has been loved off, and your eyes drop out and you get loose in the joints and very shabby. But these things don't matter at all, because once

you are Real, you can't be ugly, except to people who don't understand."

Real people *are* beautiful; and suffering, given to Christ, produces a unique beauty. But that doesn't mean it is easy.

It's all very well for me to write these things about suffering, to nod my head and say, "Yes, that's right!" Making it part of my life is something else. I find it very hard. When Jesus tells me not only to anticipate trouble but to "jump for joy" when it comes—that's a challenge. It will mean far more than nodding my head.

I think of Joachim, a man we met in a work camp in Europe many years ago. He and his family suffered the loss of many material things because he was determined to fulfill his call to preach the gospel. Joachim is a beautiful person, but his life is very difficult.

I think of our friends who, because they are Christians, are speaking out against white supremacy in a country where it is an official government policy. They are suffering as a result. In a recent letter one of them assured us, "Please believe that we are all in good heart. Our Christian faith, thank God, enables us to face persecution with equanimity and cheerfulness."

I think of the African evangelist who spoke to our congregation recently, telling us about the persecution Christians have suffered in many parts of his continent and how they were filled with forgiving love for their persecutors even in the midst of their agony.

World War II gave us some incredible examples of forgiveness. I think of Corrie ten Boom and her sister Betsie, imprisoned in the terrible concentration camp Ravens-

bruck—two brave Dutch women enduring inhuman brutal-
ity and coming through it spiritually triumphant. In *The
Hiding Place* Corrie describes her prison ordeal and the
amazing change that came into her life.

But as the rest of the world grew stranger, one
thing became increasingly clear. And that was the
reason the two of us were here. Why others should
suffer we were not shown. As for us, from morning
until lights-out, whenever we were not in ranks for
roll call, our Bible was the center of an ever-widen-
ing circle of help and hope. Like waifs clustered
around a blazing fire, we gathered about it, holding
out our hearts to its warmth and light. The blacker
the night around us grew, the brighter and truer and
more beautiful burned the word of God. "Who shall
separate us from the love of Christ? Shall tribula-
tion, or distress, or persecution, or famine, or
nakedness, or peril, or sword? . . . Nay, in all these
things we are more than conquerors through him
that loved us."

I would look about us as Betsie read, watching the
light leap from face to face. More than conquerors.
. . . It was not a wish. It was a fact. We knew it, we
experienced it minute by minute—poor, hated, hungry. We are more than conquerors. Not "we shall
be." We are! Life in Ravensbruck took place on two
separate levels, mutually impossible. One, the ob-
servable, external life, grew every day more horri-
ble. The other, the life we lived with God, grew daily
better, truth upon truth, glory upon glory.

And in that same arena, the father of Martin Niemoeller, who denied Hitler and was imprisoned, said:

> Don't let anyone pity the father and mother of Martin Niemoeller. Only pity any follower of Christ who does not know the joy that is set before those who endure the cross, depising the shame. Yes, it is a terrible thing to have a son in a concentration camp. . . . But there would be something more terrible for us: If God had needed a faithful martyr, and our Martin had been unwilling.

God met the Niemoellers and Corrie ten Boom in their time of suffering, and He will do the same for us—*whenever our cause is right.* Few of us will ever go to prison for our faith, but at some point in our lives persecution will present us with a choice: Do we enter in or back away? Do we say yes or no? Do we live or die? And by that, I don't mean only physical death, for there are other ways to die.

If we believe that the cause is right, if we are willing to suffer for the moment because God has given us eyes to see beyond now to what will follow, what then? What help will there be? What guarantee do we have that we will find strength, peace, and joy at the end of the road?

A very good friend who has known more than a little suffering in life says, "We all suffer persecution if we follow Jesus—but we must choose our hill wisely." In other words, we must be sure in our hearts that the cause we are willing to suffer for is His.

But if we believe that the cause is God's—what then?

How can we be sure He'll stand with us?

At this point I feel a little inadequate to write about this Beatitude. So many others could speak with depth of their experiences, while mine seem shallow. But Jesus doesn't tell us to seek suffering and persecution, only to expect it, accept it, and find joy in it when it comes. The portion that has come to me is small and couldn't really be called persecution, but in my times of suffering God *has* brought me a strange kind of joy, and this is what I want to share.

One day without warning, it happens—you're not looking for trouble, you don't want to make waves, but all of a sudden you have to put your faith where your mouth is. You do something that seems simple, uncompromising— and the world turns upside down.

Some years ago we moved to a new church in a very beautiful, very affluent town. The town was changing, research centers were popping up all over the area, and the state university had built a campus there. New industry brought new people, new ideas, new life-styles. Clearly, the town was on the growing edge of a changing American society. Its newness was part of what drew us there. It was also what repelled many of the established residents. That's the *where* of the situation. Add to this the *when*—the year of a bitter debate concerning open housing, which wasn't the most welcome subject in a town where there were reports of a so-called gentlemen's agreement to keep "certain elements" out. And the *who?* The new minister and his wife, who didn't have the sense to do as they were told and stay away from the controversy.

Within a short time of our installation, Louie preached

a group of sermons that applied the gospel to life—to *our* life in *our* town! In one sermon he read from Galatians 3:28: "Gone is the distinction between Jew and Greek, slave and free man, male and female—you are all one in Christ Jesus." Then he ended with a question: If we believed in this oneness, could we actually deny *anything*—housing, jobs, education—to *anyone?*

A few weeks earlier I had been asked to join an open-housing committee, and of course I did. I worked with some of our most dedicated citizens: dowagers, domestics, faculty wives, realtors, and ordinary people like me. I had no idea I was headed for trouble until one day there was a picture of our committee in the newspaper. Immediately a member of our congregation took me aside and said, "No minister's wife should ever get involved in such a controversial issue!"

Well, Louie did, and I did, and now the repercussions began. First there were phone calls from friends who felt sorry for us, then there were angry callers who wanted to put us in our place. On the Sunday Louie preached on Galatians 3:28 I just got back to the house when the phone rang; it was my first obscene call! I guess I'm pretty "cream cheese," because I was so shocked, all I could say was, "Why, sir—God bless you!" and hang up. Then there was the message telling us, "Go back to Harlem where you belong" and the endless stream of hate literature, parts of it underlined especially for us.

It went on for months. Normally I'm a mail hound, but by that time I dreaded going to the mailbox. There were other things, too: things that were hard to take, because they hit my vulnerability center, my family.

In the beginning, when Louie became aware of the hostility, he was angry. I remember walking the beach with him for hours. We were asking ourselves—and God—if this was one of those times when we were to shake the dust from our feet and move on. There were places to move on to, and certainly we were tempted, but always the sense of call and the urgency to do a job right where we were won out. Our decision was simply to seek to be faithful and take the consequences.

Then I saw something happen in Louie's life. Something was coming in from the outside. His times of quiet and prayer were rewarded with peace and love. Peace regarding what had happened, love for the opposition. It didn't seem natural—that's what I mean by "Something from outside." It was Christ's own Spirit.

I knew then that the cause was right. There would be no turning back.

It was hard to lose people because they didn't like a church that was "involved," but it was good to gain new people who wanted a church precisely because it was. It was hard to accept bigotry in some people, yet it was good to find that in some people it wasn't bigotry at all, but rather an honest difference of opinion as to the role the church is to play in the world. It was hard to be criticized by the fringes of the community, one side calling us "radical comsymps" and the other "gradualists," but it was good to sense an inner freedom that caused us to care less about what either side said. It was more important that people had the time and the opportunity to grow and change.

But all through that hard experience God was at work—and probably more in us than anywhere else. In the years since we have been pulled and pushed and made to grow, and He has been more than faithful.

God has shown us again and again that we grow most during our times of honest struggle. He has also taught us to trust Him in the dark times, even to thank Him for them.

I remember so well the first time I grappled with this paradox of gain through loss. I was also grappling with my need for a thankful heart. It was years ago, just as we were emerging from the open-housing struggle.

It happened on a rare quiet afternoon at our house. Everyone else was off somewhere, and I was about to splurge on an afternoon to myself. I was savoring the time to read. Several books I had already begun stared at me from my bed stand. I reached for the smallest one, a slim volume on praise, hoping I would have the satisfaction of finishing it. I read for most of the afternoon, and I was almost at the end of the book when a feeling of excitement came over me. I was expectant, eager, as if something important was about to happen. As I read I came to a quote from 1 Thessalonians 5:16–18 (KJV): "Rejoice evermore. Pray without ceasing. In every thing give thanks: for this is the will of God in Christ Jesus concerning you."

The words seemed to speak directly to me, and in response I began thanking God for all the beautiful and happy things in my life:

> For Louie—I thanked God for our marriage, for the mystery of loving and being one, yet separate and distinct, with room for growth.
> For our children—much younger then, but so full of

potential and joy. I almost ached with love as I
thought of Dan, Tim, Andie and Jamie.
For our extended family and our covenant brothers
and sisters.
For our congregation, our church family, and on
and on. . . .

There were so many things to thank God for. They kept
coming to my mind, one after another. I had never known
such a full heart. But when I thought I was through, the
Spirit let me know that He was not through with me. I heard
no words, but the feeling was very clear: *There is more!*

In my mind I answered, "But, Lord, I've thanked You for
everything—for *all* the good and lovely things in my life—
honestly!"

Again there was that feeling—*There is more!*

I went back to 1 Thessalonians 5:18: "In every thing give
thanks: for this is the will of God in Christ Jesus concerning
you." And again the words seemed to speak directly to me.
They weren't telling me to thank God only for the good
things. They said, "In *every* thing give thanks. . . ." All
things. Did that mean even the hard, the painful things?
Was I to thank God for the times of suffering, too? Yes, that
was the "something more." The Spirit seemed to confirm
it in my heart.

Now, if you were like me, you'd be thinking, *Wait a minute,
that would be insincere. It doesn't make sense.* To thank God
for the good that comes out of suffering is realistic—but
to thank Him for the suffering itself—well, I just didn't
understand. Yet I knew there were times when I had to
respond to God in a simple, childlike way, or my faith

wouldn't work. This was one of those times.

So I began thanking God for all the difficult experiences of the past years. One by one, I relived them, and as I named them aloud they seemed so petty: the letters, the phone calls, the looks. As God brought them into my mind I was able to let go and give them to Him—with thanks. Then it was finished, and I was spent. But I felt whole. Deep inside me something tender had been touched by a gentle, loving, healing hand.

As the burden was lifted, I felt gratitude and, finally, love. While I still didn't understand the spiritual dynamics of what had happened, I knew that thanking God in all things had done something for me that I wasn't able to do for myself. Thankfulness became the key to discovering meaning in suffering.

But Jesus promised even more than that: "Happy are those who have suffered persecution for the cause of goodness. . . ." He promised joy. Where is the joy in suffering? For me, the answer to that question brings us close to one of the mightiest truths of the faith: Christ has suffered, been wounded and bruised for *our* sake. He is with us; He understands. If He were a casual observer, it would be one thing —but to have a friend with godly compassion, One who bears our brokenness, is quite another. Jesus *shares* our suffering; He nurses us and heals us by His own wounds and stripes. As we go through our valleys, He keeps us constant company. And that is what makes the difference. His *presence* is our *joy.*

Happy is the woman who knows that God stands with her in times of suffering and persecution. When this woman is

unjustly criticized, she won't jump to her own defense; she
can take slander without lashing back; she can even accept
the misunderstanding of friends. She can do all these
things because of Christ. When there is bitterness in the
deepest parts of her heart, she asks Him to take it from her.
At that moment, when she can say, "Bless them, Lord, for
they know not what they do," the Kingdom of heaven is
hers.

10

You are the earth's salt. . . . You are the world's light.
. . .

Matthew 5:13, 14

Ye are the salt of the earth: but if the salt have lost
his savour, wherewith shall it be salted? it is thence-
forth good for nothing, but to be cast out, and to be
trodden under foot of men. Ye are the light of the
world. A city that is set on an hill cannot be hid.

Matthew 5:13, 14 KJV

Help Me Make a Difference

It is winter in Washington, finally! We have had a long,
mild fall, and only this week, the last of November, have all
the leaves fallen from the trees. Now when I look out the
windows of our three-story row house, I see the winter
silhouette: bare branches against a full, bleak sky. Certainly
not the colorful, outrageous beauty of autumn and spring.
But winter owns a beauty all its own, and I love it.

It's what I call "boot and soup" weather because I just
about live in my boots, and Louie and I just about live on
soup. A huge pot of some savory concoction simmers on a

151

back burner most of the winter, at our house, and the same pot feeds family and friends as they file through our house and end up in our old country kitchen. They tell me I make good soup, and I think I do—except when I forget the salt.

It happened just a few days ago. I had a big pot of soup brewing, and I had loaded it with good stock, herbs, and spices. Everything but the salt, which I had sitting on the sideboard, ready to start shaking and tasting. Then the phone rang, and as I hung up, as if on cue, someone knocked on the door. Much later I returned to the kitchen and absentmindedly put the salt back into the cupboard and ladled a bowl of soup for my unexpected and hungry visitor.

The guest was polite, but certainly not enthusiastic about my soup. And later, when I got around to tasting it myself, I knew why. I had left out the salt, and without it, even the good herbs and spices tasted flat. I couldn't reach for the salt fast enough. It didn't take much—just a few shakes and tastes, and the flavor began to emerge. What had been so tasteless just minutes before became full-bodied and delicious.

Salt makes a difference! And Jesus says to His followers: "You are the earth's salt."

What was He telling us? That we are to make a difference in the world?

We take so many things for granted in our world that sometimes we lose sight of their real value. Surely salt is one of these. It's essential, yet very ordinary. We see it on every table; cooks use it without even thinking. Still there must be something special, something meaningful about it.

It helps me to imagine myself back in the days when Jesus

spoke these words. Yes, already there is more substance to *salt*—for in those days you couldn't just pick up a box of salt (iodized or plain) off your supermarket shelf. Salt came from great distances, carried on the backs of camels in long caravans along dangerous routes. Since there wasn't a lot of it, it was used carefully. It was expensive, and people paid the price because no one could do without it. Salt was essential to purify, preserve, and flavor food. There were no refrigerators in those days, no tin cans or sealed packages—in fact, there wasn't very much food. And without salt, there might be starvation.

Purity, preserving, flavor—perhaps these are also the qualities of a "salty" Christian. Our "saltiness" should affect our lives—and our world—and when it doesn't, something basic is wrong.

Just today I was reading Chuck Colson's book, *Life Sentence*, and this statement hit hard, as it did when I first read it two years ago:

> A Gallup poll revealed:
> One third of all adult Americans, 50 million people, claimed to be "born again." Church attendance after a decline of 17 consecutive years was increasing. That was good news.
> Yet abortions were increasing too, at a much faster rate, divorces were up, millions of couples were living together out of wedlock, pornography was rampant, avowed homosexuals sought the right to be ordained as clergymen, economic and racial discrimination continued. The crime rate had hit an all-time record high in 1976, a subject of special

concern to me and the prison ministry of which I was
a part.

"Religion up, but morality down" was the paradox
Gallup discovered. One out of three professed to have
made a personal commitment to Christ and to be experiencing God's regenerating work, yet the world around
us was getting sicker and sicker.

"Religion is not greatly affecting our lives," Gallup con-
cluded.

What an indictment! If religion is *not* affecting our lives,
we are not "salty Christians." The Gallup poll bears out
what I recently read in a report on human rights: "In the
countries where the church is strong, they seem to have the
same problems . . . in too many cases the church has quite
comfortably accommodated itself to the national sins."
Ouch! It should not be so.

When Jesus tells us we are the earth's salt, we like that.
We take it as a compliment. But perhaps we should read on
to the warning immediately following those pleasant
words: If salt is *not* salty, it is thrown away. Perhaps Jesus
calls us salt to warn us that we can lose our flavor.

Clarence Jordan, in *The Sermon on the Mount,* writes:
"When tension ceases to exist between the church and the
world, either the world has become totally Christian, or the
church has lost its saltiness. Then the church loses its influence and is ignored."

How, then, can we hold on to our saltiness?

We can ask God to help us live a life of purity—not
perfection, but purity in motivation and direction.

Purity: In a world that has abandoned many of its moral
standards, the salty Christian will hold onto God's loving

guidelines—not because he has to, but because he wants to. He knows that God's Way is the only way to a better life.

During the past few years several young people have lived in our home—sometimes for a few days or a week, and sometimes for a year—some for happy reasons and some for sad ones. No matter who, or why, or for how long, each one left the special gift of his or her personality in our hearts. One of them, after struggling to make sense out of the changing moral values she found in her world, came to this conclusion: "Not from a sense of 'oughtness' or 'shouldness,' but from a purely practical approach, God's ways are best." She was becoming a salty Christian.

Preserving: We preserve things to keep them from rotting, from souring, from going bad. That's why Jesus wants us to be like salt rubbed into society to keep it from going bad.

How's that for a challenge! In a world like ours, where do we begin? I guess the best place is right where we are: in our homes, in our community. We have to begin by making contact with people. We have to get involved in the events that concern us. We can't hide in the church and mingle only with our Christian friends. "Christian huddles" are great for support, but not great when we insist on staying in the huddle and miss the game.

We won't always be comfortable out in the world. The rubbing in of salt may rub us, and others, the wrong way. And we must be willing to be used up. As salty Christians we cannot live surrounded by racial bigotry, exclusivism, deprivation of human rights, and exploitation of people, without shouting our protests. Of course, this brings suffering—but it also helps preserve our society and keeps us salty.

We don't have to look far to find the spots that need salt.

We will be used up, but God will use us again and again. There is no end to the supply. Our Source is inexhaustible.

Flavoring: Now, this use of salt is the easiest for me to understand. I love to cook, to spice things up, and of course I couldn't get along without salt. In fact, any complaints I get in the cooking department are usually something like, "Hey, mom, a little heavy on the salt, doncha think?" Salt brings out the flavor of food, and sometimes I overdo it. But when I use just the right amount—ah, how it enhances the meal!

Jesus said that we Christians are to be to life what salt is to food. We are to add flavor and spice, to be real people, full of fun and joy.

Robert Louis Stevenson once wrote in his journal, "Went to church today, and was not greatly depressed." Bland, flavorless people can be depressing, and Christians are the last people in the world who should be that way. We should be the happiest people because we worship a living Lord, and when the worship service is over we should carry our joy with us into our daily service out in the world.

I don't like to see blandness in the church. It makes people think that God squeezed all the fun out of the life we gave to Him. He certainly didn't. In fact, He introduces us to a deeper level of joy.

In our congregation, we have many wonderful people. I'm thinking of four widowed and retired women who call themselves "The Galloping Four," they have such fun in life and are such fun to be around. When you ask them—Mildred, Virginia, Margaret, and Bernice—if they would like to do something for fun, their response invariably is: "Yes—when?" I can still picture Virginia (we call her

Sunny, for obvious reasons) running the three-legged race with a six-year-old at our church congregational family camp, with her buddies cheering her on from the sidelines. Everyone loves being with them, and no wonder. They add flavor and zest to life wherever they go.

As I think of my four friends, I feel a wave of gratitude for the many opportunities open to women of all ages in this period of history. As God gives us courage to take risks for Him, we can dare to walk through the doors that are now open to us and let our saltiness make a difference in the world. As we learn more about ourselves, we can bring more understanding to others. As we are truly fulfilled, there is more of ourselves to give away for Christ. In my opinion there has never been a time when our saltiness can count for so much.

Though winter has definitely come to Washington, there are brief moments when the sun breaks through the dullness and the warmth is delicious. This afternoon was such a time when our daughter dropped by for a visit just as the sun broke through. We ran out on the third-floor porch and positioned ourselves where we would be drenched in the sun's healing rays. And there we sat with our eyes closed, faces upturned—mute witnesses to the fact that our California beginnings have left their mark on us.

As the sun warmed us, its light was so bright that I had to roll my head from side to side. It reminded me that Jesus also said, "You are the world's light. . . ."

Jesus, *You* are the Light of the world; yet here You are, telling us to glow. If You mean we should generate our own

light from within—well, I just can't do it. I don't have what
it takes. If I am to shine, I'll have to borrow light from You.
My life will be Your lamp.

Somewhere I read that the houses in ancient Palestine
were very dark because they each had only one small window. A lamp was simply a bowl filled with oil and a floating
wick, and it was kept on a lampstand in a prominent place
in the house. Remember, there weren't any matches in
those days, and relighting the lamp was difficult, so lamps
were left burning most of the time. When people left the
house, they placed an earthenware bushel measure over the
lamp, which allowed it to burn safely while they were away.
But when they returned, the lamp was immediately uncov-
ered so that it could bring light to everyone in the family.

That's what Jesus is telling us to do—to keep our light
in the open where it can be seen and where it can help
others to see. In other words, if we are going to live the
Beatitudes, we must do it openly, not to "be seen" of men
and women, but to serve them. This is where privacy ends.
Our light must burn brightly in our attitude toward our
fellow human beings.

Light is a powerful force that pushes back the darkness.
But there are places where light will not go. It stops at a
closed door. And so must we. We can go just so far. Some
people will resist our faith; some will run from Jesus; some
have been in darkness so long they're afraid of the Light.
It's right for us to push back the darkness, to bring God's
light out into the world, but we have to respect the closed
door. The individual will is the key to the door, and only
the person whose will it is can open it. When he does, we
can be ready to flood the area with His brightness.

Light has a nourishing quality. When I think of plants seeking the sun, I realize that light helps living things to grow. So it is with light-filled Christians who share their faith with those around them. They give food for the growing spirit.

Today there are a lot of windows in our houses. We push a button, and our homes are flooded with light—dimmer, brighter, whichever we choose. We have soft lights and highlights. Many things have changed, but we human beings are still the same. We still need the Light of the world. And we especially need Him in our homes.

How important it is for a mother and father to be light-filled Christians, to give their children an environment of warmth and nourishment where they can grow into the persons God wants them to be. How important for a husband and wife to give light to each other, for they, too, must continue to grow as loving human beings. Sometimes, when I'm weary from stretching, from growing, I see the light of my husband's faith, and it gives me energy. Hopefully my light reaches him as well.

There are others who need our light: our friends, the people we work among, our neighbors in the world. If we meet them in an attitude of love, they will grow, and so will we.

"You are the salt—You are the light." Lord, You didn't say the new church sanctuary was the light, or the church records, or the preacher. You said *you* and that's *us*.

"Let your light shine like that in the sight of men. Let them see the good things you do and praise your Father in Heaven" (Matthew 5:16). There is no better way for us to do this than to be the lamps for His light. And we become

His lamps—fitted and ready to transmit His light—by letting our lives be shaped by the Beatitudes. These are the attitudes that ought to be.

As Andie and I silently enjoyed the last few moments of the winter sun, I could feel myself smiling. I felt so rich and full. As I pondered the challenge of being a salty, light-filled follower of Jesus I became excited all over again.

Just to think that God trusts us to be *His* salt, rubbed into society, and *His* light, turned on in a darkened world, while we know this may cost us our very lives, we also know it will be our source of joy and fulfillment, for we were designed before the beginning of anything—and everything—to live for the praise of His glory.

Now the sun was gone, and immediately the air was chilled. But my heart was freshly warmed by the Spirit of God. For thirty years I had walked—sometimes stumbling —with Christ. Yet so much was still ahead, and in the goodness of that moment I somehow knew "the best is yet to be."

The everyday pressures of life demand much from you. Immerse your life in *A Deeper Joy*. You'll feel Jesus' own love and strength flow through you, enabling you to meet every day with positive, Christlike attitudes.

About the Author:

COLLEEN TOWNSEND EVANS is the wife of the Reverend Louis H. Evans, Jr., who pastors the National Presbyterian Church in Washington, D.C. She is actively involved in church and community-sponsored ministries to the poor of the inner city. Mrs. Evans is also a part-time consultant to a House Foreign Affairs subcommittee on human rights. A popular author, her books include *A New Joy, Love Is An Everyday Thing, Teaching Your Child to Pray,* and *Give Us This Day.*

)ue